S. Hrg. 113–274

FROM THE LAB BENCH TO THE COURTROOM: ADVANCING THE SCIENCE AND STANDARDS OF FORENSICS

HEARING

BEFORE THE

COMMITTEE ON COMMERCE, SCIENCE, AND TRANSPORTATION UNITED STATES SENATE

ONE HUNDRED THIRTEENTH CONGRESS

FIRST SESSION

JUNE 26, 2013

Printed for the use of the Committee on Commerce, Science, and Transportation

U.S. GOVERNMENT PRINTING OFFICE

87–927 PDF WASHINGTON : 2014

For sale by the Superintendent of Documents, U.S. Government Printing Office
Internet: bookstore.gpo.gov Phone: toll free (866) 512–1800; DC area (202) 512–1800
Fax: (202) 512–2104 Mail: Stop IDCC, Washington, DC 20402–0001

SENATE COMMITTEE ON COMMERCE, SCIENCE, AND TRANSPORTATION

ONE HUNDRED THIRTEENTH CONGRESS

FIRST SESSION

CONTENTS

FROM THE LAB BENCH TO THE COURTROOM: ADVANCING THE SCIENCE AND STANDARDS OF FORENSICS

WEDNESDAY, JUNE 26, 2013

U.S. SENATE,
COMMITTEE ON COMMERCE, SCIENCE, AND TRANSPORTATION,
Washington, DC.

The Committee met, pursuant to notice, at 2:40 p.m., in room SR–253, Russell Senate Office Building, Hon. John D. Rockefeller IV, Chairman of the Committee, presiding.

OPENING STATEMENT OF HON. JOHN D. ROCKEFELLER IV, U.S. SENATOR FROM WEST VIRGINIA

The CHAIRMAN. Apologies for being late.

We have a chance to welcome today Senator Chiesa, who was attorney general 2 days ago?

[Laughter.]

Senator CHIESA. Three weeks ago.

The CHAIRMAN. Three weeks ago.

Senator CHIESA. Yes.

The CHAIRMAN. And now you are here.

Senator CHIESA. They made me resign the same day, yep, that the Governor wrote his letter. So, yes, I am thrilled to be here. Thank you.

The CHAIRMAN. But you are not going to be here for just a day.

Senator CHIESA. I am here until October.

The CHAIRMAN. Until October? And then you are absolutely out? That is not fair.

Senator CHIESA. Out and unemployed. I don't even have a job to go back to.

[Laughter.]

The CHAIRMAN. Out and unemployed?

Senator CHIESA. Yes.

Senator THUNE. Mr. Chairman, if I might, we need to take full advantage of his expertise while he is here.

The CHAIRMAN. Yes.

Senator THUNE. And, as you mentioned, he is a former Attorney General. I want to welcome Senator Chiesa to the Committee.

The CHAIRMAN. I am sorry. That was——

Senator THUNE. No, no, no. I appreciate your willingness to welcome him here, as well.

Senator Chiesa served as Assistant U.S. Attorney in New Jersey and, of course, New Jersey Attorney General. And his experience and expertise will be of great value, because many of the subjects under the jurisdiction of our Committee are areas that he has experience in, especially on the subject that we are going to talk about today, which is an important one.

And I might add, too, Mr. Chairman, and I would warn our colleagues, that he does bring a love of sports, in particular his alma mater of Notre Dame, to the Committee. And so I suspect when we get into football season this fall, we will be hearing more from him on that subject, as well.

But, anyway, delighted to have you here, Jeff.

Senator CHIESA. Senator Thune, thank you very much. And I am still recovering from the Alabama loss, so, please——

[Laughter.]

Senator CHIESA.—nobody bring that up. Thank you.

The CHAIRMAN. Hey, you have to know something. I am the only human being in the history of this country to be on the board of the University of Notre Dame and not be a Catholic.

[Laughter.]

Senator CHIESA. We are glad to have you.

[Laughter.]

The CHAIRMAN. And it was during the Vietnam War, when everybody else was going crazy. Everybody at Notre Dame, clean-shaven, held the door open, respected people older than they were. And it all happened because Father Hesburgh sort of ran the place, right?

Senator CHIESA. He sure did. He was the president when I was there. I graduated in 1987, which was Father Hesburgh's last year as president.

The CHAIRMAN. Yes.

Senator CHIESA. And he is a towering figure there.

The CHAIRMAN. Yes. I think if they had had a board vote, I would have gotten no votes at all.

[Laughter.]

Senator CHIESA. I doubt that.

The CHAIRMAN. But I loved it. Twelve years.

Senator CHIESA. That is great.

The CHAIRMAN. I loved it.

Senator CHIESA. Terrific.

The CHAIRMAN. Again, I apologize.

Today's hearing continues a discussion that we started in the last Congress about improving the science used to catch criminals and solve crimes. And I have to tell you, I am really into this subject, and I am really happy that we are having this hearing.

But before we get to the ongoing challenges in forensic science, I would like to start with an amazing success story. It is called "DNA fingerprinting."

We have seen this incredible technology represented so many times on "CSI," et cetera, et cetera, shows that people watch, me included, and other crime shows that we take it for granted. But we shouldn't. It didn't exist 30 years ago at all. Today, it is one of our judicial system's most important tools for convicting the guilty and exonerating the innocent.

DNA fingerprinting has grown so effective and so precise that even a few cells collected from sweat, blood, or saliva can be enough to link a suspect to the crime and have it stand up, virtually non-challengeable. I am not a lawyer, but that is what my understanding is.

So this really powerful forensic technology did not develop by chance. It was the result of careful, thoughtful collaboration between the law enforcement and the scientific communities, the two of which aren't always in agreement. And I think sometimes the law enforcement community wants to keep things the way they are, and sometimes they are suspicious about science getting into the area of deciding who is the victim and who is the perpetrator and all that kind of thing.

But it was the result of a process in which technical experts developed objective measurements for determining whether DNA recovered at a crime scene precisely matched a suspect's DNA. And the word "match" is important, because there are so many words that are used now that can float back and forth and confuse things.

In a hearing held last year, this committee heard testimony from a prominent molecular geneticist, Dr. Eric Lander, who in 1989 served as an expert witness in one of the very first criminal trials to consider DNA evidence. Dr. Lander told us, during this trial, the scientific experts from the prosecution and the defense literally kicked the lawyers out—my apologies, Senator——

[Laughter.]

The CHAIRMAN.—so they could discuss the quality and validity of the DNA evidence, because it was the first shot at it.

It was discussions like these, led by independent experts, that eventually turned DNA matching into a scientific process rather than a matter of subjective professional opinion and made DNA fingerprinting the gold standard of forensic science that it is, in fact, today.

Unfortunately, the techniques used in some forensic disciplines, such as ballistics, bite mark, fingerprint analysis, et cetera, have not been subject to the rigorous scientific scrutiny that Dr. Lander and his colleagues applied to DNA matching. We now know that some of the forensic evidence presented in courtrooms proved unreliable and contributed to the wrongful conviction of innocent people.

In 2005, Congress responded to this problem by asking the National Academy of Sciences to assemble a group of experts from the law enforcement and scientific communities to take a hard look at forensic science. Now, both of those communities were in this study. Four years later, the academy sent us this book. It was their book-length report, and it is called "Strengthening Forensic Science in the United States: A Path Forward."

Most of the people in this room are familiar with the findings of this report. They demand action. The report concluded that a number of the forensic techniques used in our country today were developed and practiced, "with little foundation in scientific theory or analysis." The report called on Congress and the Federal Government to start building this missing scientific foundation.

While we have not reacted to this challenge as quickly as I would have hoped, we are beginning to make some progress. President Obama in his budget requests funding to establish a new Forensic Science Advisory Committee—there are lots of advisory committees, but maybe this will be a really important one—and increases funding for NIST's work—NIST, largely unknown to most of America but treasured in this room—their work in forensic science, and proposes to transfer funds from the Department of Justice to NIST—and my understanding is there are a few Department of Justice people here; they may not be entirely happy about that fact, if it comes to be—and the National Science Foundation to further address this problem. In other words, a pretty much all-out government assault to try to get to the basis of the science.

In the next few weeks, I will introduce an updated version of my bill submitted in the last Congress, which didn't get anywhere, S. 3378, directing our Federal science agencies to increase forensic science research and standards development useful to the law enforcement community.

Promoting truth and justice in our judicial system is a bipartisan cause, it would seem to me. And I invite all of my colleagues to look at this subject very carefully and even at the bill when it comes along.

And I call now on my distinguished, as I call him, co-Chair, Senator John Thune of the great urban state of South Dakota.

[Laughter.]

STATEMENT OF HON. JOHN THUNE, U.S. SENATOR FROM SOUTH DAKOTA

Senator THUNE. Thank you, Mr. Chairman. And thanks for holding this hearing. This hearing, as you said, examines the state of forensic science and related standards and the challenges facing the forensic science community.

Popular television shows like "CSI," "NCIS," and "Law and Order," to name a few which I know the chairman TiVos, have showcased the role that forensic science can play in helping law enforcement carry out investigations and convict criminals. However, these shows can also create the misimpression that all courtroom evidence that is presented as scientific evidence has been subjected to high-tech, foolproof analysis and that every state and local crime lab around the country has easy access to these sophisticated lab technologies. Unfortunately, this is not always the case. A National Academies report issued 4 years ago raised serious concerns about the state of forensic science and, among other things, called for structural reforms in new research.

While the forensic science community did not embrace all of the report's reform recommendations, there seems to be general agreement that law enforcement, prosecutors, and crime labs would benefit from greater research and training efforts to increase crime lab capacity and accuracy and to strengthen the scientific foundations of forensic science. For instance, advances in forensic DNA analysis have improved the strength of evidence that can put criminals behind bars and also clear the innocent.

However, as we explore ways to improve forensic science, we must be careful not to undermine or threaten the ability of local prosecutors and other law enforcement professionals to prosecute cases by fostering unrealistic expectations that every case can be solved through science.

We must also avoid unintentionally and undeservedly casting doubt on the good work that the vast majority of practitioners perform. Federal efforts to improve forensic science should utilize input from and be cognizant of the needs of state and local practitioners in both the forensic and law enforcement fields.

I would like to hear today about the extent of involvement of state and local practitioners in the National Commission on Forensic Science recently established by the administration. Along those same lines, I would like to hear the witnesses' views about how to best leverage existing Federal efforts and longstanding partnerships with state and local forensic scientists to improve forensic sciences.

I also look forward to hearing your thoughts about what the National Institute of Standards and Technology, NIST, under this Committee's jurisdiction, could do to advance forensic science standards and how the Department of Justice and NIST could best work together to enhance both public safety and confidence in our system of justice.

So I look forward to hearing the testimony of our witnesses today. I would also like to thank all of the witnesses for being here, some of whom have flown in from across the country and even from abroad.

So thank you, Mr. Chairman.

The CHAIRMAN. Thank you, Senator Thune, very much.

What I would like to do is just have each of you give your statements. And, incidentally, don't be depressed by looking around here and not seeing—I mean, the three of us are pretty good.

[Laughter.]

The CHAIRMAN. But there are eight more senators who have said they are going to be here. And I have them written down right here, so Senator Thune and I will be observing that list and those appearances closely.

[Laughter.]

The CHAIRMAN. Dr. Tjark Tsin-A-Tsoi is a Ph.D., Chief Executive Officer of the Netherlands Forensic Institute.

You will be the first to speak, but let me introduce each of you.

Mr. Michael Bromwich, who is Managing Principal of The Bromwich Group, LLC; Partner, Goodwin Procter, LLP; former Inspector General, Department of Justice.

Dr. Gregory Schmunk, President, National Association of Medical Examiners, Chief Medical Examiner.

And Ms. Jill Spriggs, Secretary, Consortium of Forensic Science Organizations; Laboratory Director, Office of the District Attorney, Sacramento County Laboratory of Forensic Services.

So, Doctor, if you wish to go ahead, please do so.

Well, you are all doctors.

[Laughter.]

The CHAIRMAN. You, sir.

STATEMENT OF DR. T. (TJARK) B.P.M. TJIN-A-TSOI, CHIEF EXECUTIVE OFFICER, NETHERLANDS FORENSIC INSTITUTE

Mr. TJIN-A-TSOI. Good afternoon, Chairman Rockefeller and Ranking Member Thune and members of the Committee. It is an honor for me, as Chief Executive Officer of the Netherlands Forensic Institute, to be invited here to testify before your committee on the important topic of forensic sciences.

New science and technology are transforming the capabilities of forensic laboratories. As a result of this, forensic science is changing from having a supporting role to becoming a playmaker in criminal investigations and security.

The promise of forensic science is that it will increasingly enable quick and reliable reconstructions of events, as well as the identification of subjects, through scientifically validated means. Furthermore, it will do so in a relatively cost-effective way, with minimal impact on innocent civilians.

As such, forensic sciences are set to play a role similar to chemistry and biology in health care and automation in manufacturing. However, in order to live up to that promise, the sector still has some challenges to overcome. These challenges are a result of the way forensic science and crime labs have developed over the years.

An important challenge concerns the scientific validity of the methods used by forensic scientists to interpret evidence, as was discussed in the 2009 National Academy of Sciences report.

Scientific research is essential to strengthen the objectivity of forensic interpretations and to determine the strengths and limitations of forensic methods. This is the background of the MOU the National Institutes of Standards and Technology and the Netherlands Forensics Institute signed in November 2012.

Furthermore, through scientific research, the sector can move toward more integrated, interdisciplinary information services aimed not only at identifying the source of traces but also at reconstructing the human events that led up to them, the human activities that led up to them.

The second challenge concerns the strong technology-driven growth of the forensic sector during the past 2 decades, even in jurisdictions where the crime rate has been falling. Forensic sciences are increasingly becoming mission-critical from the point of view of end-users. Nevertheless, the forensic community and its stakeholders have been struggling to deal with this, essentially, very good success.

In the absence of adequate mechanisms to coordinate supply and demand and in view of a somewhat reserved attitude in the sector toward professionalization of governance and process management, demand growth has resulted in backlogs and long delivery times in many labs around the world. These backlogs stand in the way of delivering the full value of forensic sciences to users and obstruct the scientific development of the field as a whole.

The Netherlands Forensic Institute, which is an independent and not-for-profit government agency with approximately 650 employees, was facing the same problem 6 years ago. The policy paper that is in your possession describes the journey of the NFI over the past 6 years. In this period, the NFI changed its governance and business model, which involved shaping a more realistic and businesslike relationship with its end-users and other stakeholders.

These changes have resulted in the elimination of the entire backlog of 18,000 cases, a reduction of the average delivery time of more than 90 percent, and customer satisfaction levels that are now comparable to the private sector. As the weight of backlogs was lifted, the ability to initiate research and development programs was enhanced, as well.

Even though some of these changes initially went against the grain of the stakeholder network in which forensic laboratories operate, in the end the results were welcomed universally.

Finally, I would like to discuss a topic that is related to all the aforementioned issues. It concerns the organizational fragmentation of forensic infrastructure. Not only is there much to be gained if the dozens of different fields of expertise were to cooperate more intensively, the organizational structure of the sector is such that there is a large number of relatively small and local labs that are managed separately.

Fragmentation tends to have the effect that economy of scale and scope are not achieved and renders expensive R&D programs impossible due to the absence of critical mass. Furthermore, it often gives rise to problems relating to flexibility and continuity. Partly because of this, most forensic laboratories around the world operate like pure production units, even though they have the knowledge and the customer exposure that could propel forensic sciences forward.

For that reason, consolidation, specialization, or more formalized cooperation agreements could be considered in order for the field to utilize its full potential and develop new capabilities.

Thank you for your attention, and I am happy to answer any questions you might have.

[The prepared statement of Mr. Tjin-A-Tsoi follows:]

PREPARED STATEMENT OF DR. T. (TJARK) B.P.M. TJIN-A-TSOI, CHIEF EXECUTIVE OFFICER, NETHERLANDS FORENSIC INSTITUTE

Good afternoon Chairman Rockefeller, Ranking Member Thune and members of the Committee. It is an honor for me, as Chief Executive Officer of the Netherlands Forensic Institute, to be invited here to testify before your committee on the important topic of forensic sciences.

New science and technology are transforming the capabilities of forensic laboratories. As a result of this, forensic science is changing from having a supporting role to becoming a playmaker in criminal investigations and security. The promise of forensic sciences is that it will increasingly enable quick and reliable reconstructions of events, as well as the identification of suspects, through scientifically validated means. Furthermore, it will do so in a relatively cost effective way, with minimal impact on innocent civilians.

As such, forensic sciences are set to play a role similar to chemistry and biology in health care, and automation in manufacturing.

However, in order to live up to that promise, the sector still has some challenges to overcome. These challenges are a result of the way forensic sciences and crime labs have developed over the years.

An important challenge concerns the *scientific validity* of the methods used by forensic scientists to interpret evidence, as was discussed in a well-known 2009 *National Academy of Sciences* report. Scientific research is essential to strengthen the *objectivity* of forensic interpretations and to determine the *strengths and limitations* of forensic methods. This is the background of the Memorandum of Understanding (MoU) the National Institute of Standards and Technology and the Netherlands Forensic Institute signed in November 2012.

Furthermore, through scientific research, the sector can move towards more integrated and interdisciplinary *information services,* aimed not only at identifying the *source* of traces but also at reconstructing the human *activities* that led up to them.

The second challenge concerns the strong *technology driven growth* of the forensic sector during the past two decades, even in jurisdictions where crime rates have been falling. Forensic sciences are increasingly becoming *mission critical* from the point of view of end users. Nevertheless, the forensic community and its stakeholders have struggled to deal with what is essentially an enormous success. In the absence of adequate mechanisms to coordinate supply and demand, and in view of a somewhat reserved attitude in the sector towards professionalization of governance and process management, demand growth has resulted in *backlogs* and *long delivery times* in many labs around the world. These backlogs stand in the way of delivering the full value of forensic sciences to users, and obstruct the scientific development of the field as a whole.

The Netherlands Forensic Institute, which is an independent and not-for-profit government agency with approximately 650 employees, was facing the same problems six years ago. The policy paper that is in your possession describes the journey of the NFI over the past six years. In this period the NFI changed its governance and business model, which involved shaping a more realistic and businesslike relationship with its end users and other stakeholders. These changes have resulted in the elimination of the entire backlog of 18,000 cases, a reduction of the average delivery time by over 90 percent, and customer satisfaction levels that are now comparable to the private sector. As the weight of backlogs was lifted, the ability to initiate research and development programs was enhanced as well.

Even though some of the changes initially went against the grain of the stakeholder network in which forensic laboratories operate, in the end the results were welcomed universally.

Finally, I would like to discuss a topic that is related to all the aforementioned issues. It concerns the organizational fragmentation of the forensic infrastructure. Not only is there much to be gained if the dozens of different fields of expertise were to cooperate more intensively, the organizational structure of the sector is such that there is a large number of relatively small and local labs, that are managed separately. Fragmentation tends to have the effect that economy of scale and scope are not achieved, and renders expensive R&D programs impossible due to the absence of critical mass. Furthermore, it often gives rise to problems relating to flexibility and continuity. Partly because of this, most forensic laboratories around the world operate like pure production units, even though they have the knowledge and customer exposure that could propel forensic sciences forward. For that reason, consolidation, specialization, or more formalized cooperation arrangements could be considered, in order for the field to utilize its full potential and develop new capabilities.

Thank you for your attention and I am happy to answer any questions you might have.

March 2013

TRENDS, CHALLENGES AND STRATEGY IN THE FORENSIC SCIENCE SECTOR

Dr. T.B.P.M. Tjin-A-Tsoi, Chief Executive Officer, Netherlands Forensic Institute [1]

Introduction

The forensic science sector is in transition. New insights, technologies, and customers, combined with falling costs and increasing capabilities cause the sector to grow rapidly. As a consequence the role of forensic laboratories is changing. Today's laboratories are able to investigate more and a greater variety of traces, and to extract more information from less material, than ever before. Forensic IT [2] has opened a completely new category of investigation, as specialists explore digital traces on information carriers such as cell phones, laptops, and car computers. Meanwhile, advances in the study of DNA have made it possible to investigate minute traces and even provide information on the physical characteristics of the donor. In addition, all this information can now be produced more quickly than was ever thought possible. Due to these developments, rapid and well-founded reconstructions of events based on trace patterns found at crime scenes are becoming a tantalizing possibility. And these advantages come at a lower cost than many conventional investigative techniques.

As a result, the role of forensic science is changing. Whereas before, it was cast in a supporting role, it is now set to become the playmaker in many types of investigation, providing quick and reliable information on scenarios and suspects and thus, in a sense, directing the efforts of investigators. At the same time, forensics is changing from a profession in which individual experience and expertise of practitioners play a dominant role to one where skilled knowledge workers are integrated in an increasingly complex infrastructure of empirical science and cutting-edge technology.

Taking advantage of these developments to achieve the full potential of the forensic sector will naturally require some adjustment. Despite the sector's rapid growth

[1] The Netherlands Forensic Institute is an independent and not-for-profit government agency. It is part of the Ministry of Security and Justice.

[2] Forensic Information Technology

in recent years, its structure remains largely unchanged. With more than 400 forensic laboratories in the U.S. alone and a somewhat smaller, but still very large, number in Europe, it is a rather fragmented field. Most of these laboratories are primarily production units that lack sufficient mass or funding to conduct research, or to develop innovative products and services. Furthermore, this lack of critical mass creates major organizational vulnerabilities, which are in part responsible for the backlogs that haunt many forensic laboratories.

This paper presents an overview, from the standpoint of the Netherlands Forensic Institute (NFI), of some of the trends and pressures that will affect the structure and governance of the sector today and in the years to come. The paper also outlines a way forward, based on measures that the NFI has itself taken to address these challenges.

1. Growth—one of the main trends in forensics today

One of the clearest and most important trends in forensics is its remarkable growth over the past 15 years. At the NFI, the number of cases handled per year is now six times what it was in 2000. In fact, the caseload has grown more in the past 15 years than in the previous 50. In the same period, the NFI's workforce has nearly tripled, growing from about 200 to 600 people. This is clearly part of a larger trend, with caseloads growing steadily at forensic laboratories around the world. Although the recent budget cuts and the economic downturn may temporarily slow the growth of the forensic sector, the fundamental drivers of change persist and will continue to assert themselves.

Factors driving growth

The growth in forensics has been driven by three main factors: (1) the introduction of new technological capabilities, (2) increased general awareness among customers regarding the value and efficiency of forensic science, and (3) the advent of new types of customers from outside the scope of traditional forensics. Let us look at these factors in turn.

New technological capabilities

Much of the recent growth in forensics has resulted from the introduction of new technologies, most notably high-tech biometrics (predominantly forensic DNA), forensic information technology (IT), and forensic chemistry. Just twenty years ago, the first two of these disciplines were not practiced at the NFI; today, they are the largest and fastest growing disciplines at the Institute.

That these new technologies should lead to growth is not surprising. When any new investigative technique is introduced, the pressure to put it into practice quickly increases. Of course, in forensics—as in other fields (*e.g.,* health care)—ethical and quality issues may need to be resolved before a new technique can be used. Otherwise, if it provides valuable information, there will be a strong demand for it to be used immediately and on a wide scale. Since, in this way, any new scientific insight or technology creates its own demand, forensic innovations are likely to continue to spur growth in the field.

It is significant that the three disciplines mentioned above (forensic DNA, IT, and chemistry) do not simply add new and refined technological capabilities to the forensics toolbox. They also address new classes of trace evidence—classes that previously may not have been collected and analyzed. This applies both to biometrics and to forensic IT, but the discipline of forensic IT is particularly significant in this context, as it opens up a whole new world of trace evidence. Today, it is almost impossible to prevent leaving digital traces—in cell phones, on computers, on the Internet, in digital surveillance cameras, in an ATM, in a navigation system, in a car's on-board computer, and so on. People have a symbiotic relationship with both the physical and the digital world. This has profound consequences for forensics, because everything we do leaves a trace in these worlds. It will therefore become increasingly important that forensic service providers be able to retrieve relevant data from all available digital sources and to analyze these intelligently.

Of course, additional growth is also generated through the continuous improvement of existing technologies. As they become more sensitive, the amount of relevant information that can be retrieved from traces will increase, as will the number of traces that can be analyzed in the first place. For example, 15 years ago, a relatively large sample was needed for reliable forensic DNA analysis. Today, forensic laboratories need just a fraction of that: often no more than 50 picograms. Traces that in the past would have yielded no relevant information can now change the course of an investigation.

Moreover, advances in technology mean that forensic laboratories are able to do much more with the same resources (in money terms) than before—so that the value of the laboratory as a whole has increased significantly.

Greater awareness of the value, efficiency and potential of forensics

The use of forensic investigations has increased not only due to the advent of new technologies but also due to an increased awareness of what forensics has to offer. Existing and potential end-users, the press and the public are all more aware today of the extent of forensic capabilities. This, in turn, is generating an increasing demand. Forensic investigation is gradually assuming a more central and high-profile role, and is becoming an essential tool for law enforcement, homeland defense, and others entrusted with maintaining justice, social order and security. Increasingly, court cases depend on DNA evidence, security and terrorism threats are being prevented on the basis of digital traces, and a wide variety of investigators are taking an interest in what forensics has to offer them.

Historically, forensic science has served primarily as the tool of prosecutors in preparation for trial, not necessarily as a tool of investigators. With the advent of faster methods and forensic databases (DNA, fingerprints, firearms, etc.) over the past several decades, forensic science is becoming an invaluable tool in criminal investigations and intelligence, even before a suspect has been identified. For example, investigators can now compare questioned traces collected from crime scenes or victims with large database pools of known perpetrators, frequently leading to the identification of suspects who would otherwise remain unknown.

As users become more aware of the benefits of the new tools and expertise available, they see new ways to use forensic science. For example, the police are under great pressure to apprehend criminals while at the same time ruling out innocent civilians as suspects. Forensics can help them meet that need by providing reliable information through technical means (*i.e.,* without harassing innocent citizens). This increased awareness of what advanced forensics has to offer is leading to increased demand on the part of traditional customers of forensics laboratories.

New customers

The capabilities of forensic service providers have not passed unnoticed in domains outside of criminal justice and law enforcement. In fact, a wide range of governmental organizations—involved in everything from defense and intelligence to administrative law and regulatory oversight—are using forensics in their investigations. This new demand for forensic science is a main driver of growth in the sector as a whole. Nevertheless, not many traditional crime labs are taking advantage of this fact.

Of course, new customers have different needs from those within the criminal justice system (police, prosecutors and the judiciary). For example, the type of information required and the balance between speed and accuracy may be quite different. Accordingly, in recent years, many of these organizations have created their own specialized forensic units and, in some organizations, their own databases. However, these units are often small and somewhat disconnected from the wider forensic community. This has increased the fragmentation of the forensics sector as a whole, and has occasionally resulted in some organizations "reinventing the wheel." Nonetheless, these changes also represent an opportunity for the forensic sector. Serving a broader customer base not only reduces organizational vulnerability, but can also give rise to improved services at lower costs through economies of scale. The atypical requirements of new types of customers stimulate innovation and drive the development of new knowledge, which will ultimately benefit all customers.

As a result of these shifts, a new outlook of the forensic community is emerging. It no longer solely provides forensic services in the fields of law enforcement and criminal justice. Forensic institutes become first and foremost high-tech knowledge hubs, filled with knowledge workers who deliver their services to the (mostly government) agencies that may require these and who enrich the hub in the process. At the NFI, this process could be observed at first hand: by serving non-traditional customers, inside and outside of the Netherlands in 17 countries (at the time of writing), the organization has acquired capabilities and experience that it would not otherwise have been able to obtain, and that are now also available to "traditional" customers. As knowledge hubs, forensic institutes become more valuable if they enlarge the network to which they belong and in which the operate.

Non-traditional customers include ministries of defense, municipalities, intelligence agencies, benefit and tax fraud investigators, the financial market regulator, transport safety boards, competition authorities, and international bodies, such as the international tribunals and criminal courts, but also Europol, Interpol, the IAEA, and the United Nations.

2. Customer focus

The current heightened awareness of forensic science, together with the recognition of its value, means that users and customers not only make greater use of it, but also place greater reliance on it. In short, forensics has moved from occupying a supporting—almost behind-the-scenes—role to becoming a key protagonist. It has, for many users, become "mission critical." As a result, customers are becoming increasingly demanding, subjecting what they receive from their suppliers to ever-closer scrutiny. Consequently, suppliers will need to pay much more attention to their customers' needs.

Identifying customers' primary needs

Forensic laboratories supply their customers with "value-added" information—specifically, about past events and behaviors, as well as about the individuals involved in these events. This information is obtained from the traces that resulted from these events and behaviors. All customers want the supplier laboratory to provide as much relevant information from available traces as possible, and they want the information to be reliable and objective. They do not want the information to depend on the particular forensic investigator handling the case; and, if necessary, they want the forensic investigators to be able to show a solid scientific basis for their conclusions.

Customers also want the laboratory to be able to handle as many trace investigations as possible, because in general (though not always) a larger number of trace investigations yields more information. It also reduces the risk, down the line, that police investigators or prosecutors will be criticized for failing to order trace investigations that are potentially exculpatory, or for failing to do everything possible to apprehend the criminals. When forensic laboratories have a fixed budget, the drive to increase the total output of the laboratory implies that the average cost per investigation has to be reduced.

To most customers of forensic laboratories, receiving the results of the forensic investigation as quickly as possible is extremely important. This is especially true in the intelligence gathering and investigation phases, when time is of the essence. After a crime has been committed, the first 48 hours are often critical in the investigation. In the intelligence phase, being able to analyze traces quickly and reliably can mean the difference between being able to prevent a crime (such as a terrorist attack) or not. The value and impact of forensics increase greatly when results can be delivered quickly.

In other words, the primary needs of the customer can be summarized as follows: more, better, faster, cheaper. In fact, "more", "faster" and "cheaper" are highly correlated from an organizational and governance point of view, as will be discussed below. The forensic community has historically paid less passionate attention to these customer needs than to the technical content of the forensic trades and the individual skills of the practitioners. In most cases, the costs of individual forensic investigations are not considered at all, either directly or indirectly. Many forensic investigators, laboratory directors, and even customers, actually resist the idea that costs should play any role in the decision-making process before committing to forensic investigations. The implicit belief seems to be that one cannot and should not let financial considerations play such a key role when important societal issues (such as apprehending a criminal and dispensing justice) are at stake. However, since open-ended financial arrangements are an illusion, the practical results of this way of thinking are backlogs, stagnation, and a far-from-optimal—even unknowing—allocation of scarce resources.

All this is changing, however, and will continue to change due to the increasing reliance on forensic investigations and the pressure this puts on forensic laboratories. The same can be said about the drive to increase the information value extracted from traces, as well as the scientific basis and objectivity of forensic conclusions. Both require focused and customer-oriented research and development. However, at the moment, partly because of the arts-and-crafts culture of the forensic field, and partly because of the fragmented structure of the sector (see the previous section), there is a lack of R&D of this type.

Achieving more, better, and more valuable information

Forensic laboratories can increase the value of the information they provide in at least three ways. The first is by increasing reliability by strengthening objectivity and scientific underpinning. The second is by providing more information at "activity" level, *i.e.,* information that reveals how traces fit together in larger patterns of crime related activity. Finally, laboratories can enhance the information they offer by developing tools and methods that bring to light traces that have hitherto been unavailable because they are imperceptible to the human senses.

Improving scientific underpinning—Up to just a few decades ago, forensic science had more in common with a collection of arts and crafts than with a mature science. In some areas, forensics is essentially still in the pre-scientific era, a fact reflected in the observation by the National Academy of Sciences (NAS) that some forensic disciplines lack a scientific basis.[3] Clearly, if the interpretations made by forensic scientists are not objective or lack a strong scientific underpinning, the value of the information and interpretations forensic labs provide is diminished. The arts-and-crafts culture, the small scale of most forensic laboratories, and the high pressure on throughput, have had the result that the scientific and technological development of the field have not been as rapid as it could have been. In addition, knowledge is often not shared and managed, but resides with skilled, individual practitioners. In essence, these professionals become their own measuring instruments, and the database from which they operate and evaluate forensic evidence is based on personal experience. Consequently, interpretations are more subjective than is often realized. To a certain extent, this is probably unavoidable, but it would be too easy to say that it is *entirely* unavoidable. With empirical scientific research, it should be possible to strengthen the scientific basis of many forensic disciplines.

Providing activity-level information—A second way in which laboratories can increase the value of the information they deliver is to provide customers with more information at "activity" level. Many forensic laboratories restrict themselves to "source level" investigations, focusing on the origin and composition of a given trace. However, from the point of view of the customer, it is also important how and when the trace was made; *i.e.,* what events transpired to leave a certain trace (or pattern of traces). In the case of DNA and latent fingerprints found at a crime scene, for instance, it would be useful to know not only to whom the DNA or latent fingerprints belong, but also what activity led to the evidence being deposited there. Was it an activity related to the crime, or was it entirely unrelated? So far, relatively little research has been carried out to increase the capabilities of forensic investigations at activity level. In those cases where forensic practitioners have included some analysis at activity level in their reports, it is often based on the practitioner's particular experience, rather than any empirical scientific research. However, the added value provided by activity-level information suggests that such research is highly desirable. It is, however, expensive, time-consuming, and requires substantial case-loads to be able to create the necessary empirical databases. Critical mass and cooperation among laboratories are both essential in this regard.

Detecting, recording, and retrieving minute traces—A third way in which laboratories can increase the value of the information they provide to customers is to gain access to traces left at the crime scene that are currently too small to detect with the human senses. Detecting such traces is becoming a new "holy grail" of forensics. Although it is currently possible to investigate such minute traces in the laboratory, it is still impossible (within a reasonable timeframe) to detect, register and represent all these important traces not merely in isolation but also in the three-dimensional patterns in which they occur at the crime scene. It may be possible to investigate 50 picograms of cell material containing DNA in the laboratory, but how does one find such small quantities at a crime scene? This is certainly an important R&D challenge. (Incidentally, it should be noted that the growing numbers of traces that will become available in this way make it all the more important that forensic laboratories take steps to increase their efficiency and productivity, because increased numbers of traces will steadily increase the caseload: see below.)

Shortening delivery times

As was discussed above, quick delivery is one of the most important needs that customers of forensic laboratories articulate. In fact, as forensic investigations are increasingly becoming "mission critical" to customers, forensic laboratories have to reconcile themselves to the fact that customers—if given the choice—would like the results immediately. This does not mean that customers in all circumstances *need* the results immediately, or that they are always in a position to act on the information the moment it is provided. However, regardless of how fast investigators are able to act on the laboratory's results, it is a laudable goal for forensic laboratories to reduce the odds of being the choke point in the critical path of criminal investigations. Furthermore, suppliers (forensic laboratories in this case) usually do not have all the information necessary to determine what is important to the customer, and there may be subjective or even emotional (but not necessarily irrelevant) reasons

---

[3] *Strengthening Forensic Science in the United States: A Path Forward, NAS,* 2009: "The simple reality is that the interpretation of evidence is not always based on scientific studies to determine its validity. This is a serious problem. Although research has been done in some disciplines, there is a notable dearth of peer-reviewed, published studies establishing the scientific bases and validity of many forensic methods" . . . "The fact is that many forensic tests have never been exposed to stringent scientific scrutiny. Most of these techniques were developed in crime laboratories to aid the investigation of evidence from a particular crime scene, and researching their limitations and foundations was never a top priority."

why customers want fast delivery. However, historically the sense of urgency felt by customers regarding fast delivery was not always shared fully by the forensic community. The NFI was no exception. However, as will be discussed below, the problem is not caused exclusively by a lack of focus on speed by forensic laboratories. It is also caused by the institutional arrangements and financing structures in which the forensic sector operates.

There are at least three ways in which delivery times can be shortened: by solving the backlog problem; by improving process management; and by creating new, faster technologies.

The backlog problem—Two factors that have a significant impact on the caseload of forensic laboratories are the crime rate and the scientific and technological capabilities of the laboratories. The way in which the crime rate impacts forensic laboratories is similar to the way it influences the broader law enforcement community. However, the impact of scientific progress and technological innovation is far more complicated, and clearly sets forensic labs apart from their main customers. Advances in forensic technology tend to increase the caseload of laboratories—sometimes dramatically—even when the crime rate is going down. Conversely, to some extent powerful forensic techniques replace more "traditional" and time-consuming investigative methods, or at a minimum can provide more focus to a criminal investigation. These phenomena could be clearly observed in The Netherlands, where the crime rate has gone down in the past decade, while the number of cases the NFI handles has increased by a factor of six. This increase is almost exclusively confined to the forensic fields that have experienced significant technological advances. The largest increase in demand has been witnessed in forensic DNA analysis, forensic IT, and forensic chemistry. However, more recently, technological and scientific advances in other fields—such as new fingermark detection methods and the evaluation of partial fingermarks—have also had the effect of greatly increasing the demand in these fields. As soon as new, powerful and validated forensic techniques become available, customers want to use them in their criminal investigations.

These "technology-driven" demand shocks, during which the demand for certain forensic services increases quickly, are often not adequately factored into the budgetary models used to allocate resources to the different entities within the law enforcement community (if such models exist at all). Forensic laboratories are usually not paid for the amount of work they are commissioned to do (the demand), but are instead given a fixed budget that is supposed to cover all the work sent to them. An increase in demand caused, for example, by an innovative forensic method, does not automatically lead to a commensurate increase in financing, which could then be invested to create additional production capacity. Conversely, demand is not tempered by a "fee", and most labs do not have production agreements (*i.e.,* Service Level Agreements) with their customers, limiting the amount of work that can be commissioned. Forensic investigations cost money—sometimes a lot of money—but the parties commissioning these investigations are often not conscious of this fact. For them, the forensic investigations are "free", and they behave as if there are no budgetary or capacity constraints. This is the double-edged sword that has created backlogs all over the world. Due to the existing institutional arrangements and funding structures, budgets are not adjusted quickly enough when demand shocks present themselves, and customers are not disciplined by any kind of fee structure, or production agreements, that signal to them that forensic investigations cost money and that resources are limited. The inevitable result of this is a backlog. The fields that are hardest hit are often those that are most dynamic and that show the most scientific and technological progress. The huge DNA backlogs in many forensic laboratories around the world are an illustration of this phenomenon.

When resources are limited, as is invariably the case, prioritization becomes a necessity. However, the fact that forensic services are treated as if they were "free of charge" robs customers of the opportunity to evaluate costs versus potential benefits, given the fact that resources are limited. The inevitable result is that scarce resources are not being used in the most efficient and effective way, and significant waste is occurring even as backlogs pile up.

Some may object (for a variety of reasons) to any notion of "charging" for forensic investigations. This is perhaps in part because they fear commercialization. However, what is being discussed here is not some sort of commercialization scheme, but rather a more efficient allocation method, *i.e.,* one that prevents backlogs and waste, and leads to more informed and conscious prioritization mechanisms. It requires a repudiation of the double illusion that forensic investigations cost nothing and that forensic laboratories have unlimited capacity. It does not necessitate the establishment of any for-profit entity. Indeed, given the large number of cases that pass through forensic laboratories each month, it is neither practical nor necessary for them to start sending out bills for every investigation completed. This would create a huge and undesirable bureaucracy between agencies. An easier way—and one that has been implemented at the NFI—is to reach an annual agreement with the main customers on the number of forensic services (of different types) that the laboratory will deliver during the following year. The total "fee" of these SLAs is then equal to the agreed budget for the laboratory. Any additional work is fee based and requires separate agreements.[4]

Improving process management—Historically, the field of forensic science is a collection of communities of craftsmen and highly educated experts in a large number of different fields. Forensic laboratories often contain many different forensic disciplines (more than 30 at the NFI) and sometimes tend to resemble a collection of fiefdoms. Deep interdisciplinary cooperation is relatively rare, and individualism is an often-dysfunctional part of the culture. Practitioners in the field of forensic science are highly committed, closely focused on the content and quality of their work and, in general, not particularly interested in process management, efficiency, delivery times, costs, or other matters of this nature. Because of this, process optimization has been somewhat neglected, resulting in practices that are often less efficient than they should be.

By applying modern process redesign methods, spectacular progress can be made towards faster delivery times, higher productivity, and lower costs. Process redesign can also help with backlog reduction. Many of these methods are data-driven and quantitative, which means that natural scientists and engineers can relate to the methodology. To restructure and improve the processes at the NFI, the methodology known as "Lean Six Sigma"[5] has been introduced. A large number of employees (up to a third of the total workforce) were trained in basic or advanced process redesign skills, so that process management became part of the culture and vocabulary of the organization, rather than an unpopular instrument imposed by management.

Creating faster technologies—Many forensic laboratories are not active in R&D or product development, while those that are tend to focus on exploring scientific matters or improving existing techniques. R&D specifically aimed at faster production is relatively rare. Nevertheless, significant gains can be made by refocusing R&D more closely on techniques and methods that will accelerate processing.

Experiences at the NFI

Like many other forensic institutes around the world, the NFI used to have a significant backlog problem. However, the organization has now successfully implemented a number of the measures described above, with the result that the backlog has been eliminated. The following section describes three of these measures in more detail: introducing Service Level Agreements (SLAs) with customers; process redesign to streamline production; and refocusing R&D activities to focus on speed.

Introducing SLAs with customers

The first strategic measure implemented by the NFI was to introduce an annual SLA with its two main customers (the police and the prosecution service). This is a formal document defining the working relationship between the NFI and the customer, and specifying the number of investigations the NFI will carry out for that specific customer over a period of one year.

An important advantage of an SLA is that it forces customers to prioritize. Some people in the field implicitly believe that prioritizing among investigations is unethical, as being somehow incompatible with the notion that Justice should be blind. Nevertheless, even if justice is blind and all cases are equally important, the same cannot be said of forensic investigations if they are considered in the specific contexts of the cases in which they arise. A forensic investigation that is crucial in case *A* may be unnecessary in case *B*. Furthermore, the fact remains that the capacity of a forensic laboratory is limited, and any work that is assigned beyond that level will, under a "no-prioritization policy", simply increase the backlog and extend delivery times. In practice, it is impossible to avoid prioritization: if the customer does not do so explicitly, it will be done implicitly and therefore ad hoc. Work will be de facto prioritized on the basis of "first come, first served". From the point of view of the public good and society's needs, this is surely a situation that is far from ideal.

The SLA makes it clear that resources are limited, and that intelligent prioritization is required. Prioritization of investigations is the responsibility of the customer,

[4] For jurisdictions in which the implementation of fee structures is simply not an available option, the creation of service level agreements can still be one of the most effective ways to manage supply and demand. Nevertheless, in order to link service levels (supply) and budgets, one still needs a way to calculate the cost of the services delivered.

[5] Michael L. George, *Lean Six Sigma: Combining Six Sigma Quality with Lean Speed,* McGraw-Hill Osbourne Media, 2002

as the customer is naturally most familiar with the various cases and the relative urgency of the forensic investigations being considered. In practice, this is performed, when necessary, by liaison officers of the main customers. The step from capacity to budgets is made by modern cost accounting methods, such as *Activity-Based Costing,* which allows the organization to calculate the costs of individual investigations. In the Netherlands, the total "fee" for the work specified in the SLA is paid by the Dutch Ministry of Security and Justice, which also owns the NFI.

The SLA, which is "renegotiated" annually, prevents the accumulation of a backlog, and gives the customer an opportunity to stipulate requirements regarding important issues such as quality, logistics, and communication. This mutual formalization of the relationship gives both parties a better understanding of what is required, what they can expect and what is attainable. At first there was considerable pushback regarding the idea of introducing an SLA. However, once the logic was internalized and the advantages became apparent, it became an accepted and valuable instrument to improve a system that had created a backlog of 18,000 cases, and which had led to many instances of friction because of unclear mutual expectations.

Customers whose investigations are not paid for by the Ministry of Security and Justice pay a fee for the products or services they require. Furthermore, if the police or the prosecution request more investigations than are covered by the SLA, they pay for the additional work out of their own funds. The extra revenue that the NFI generates in this way is transparently re-invested in additional capacity and R&D. In this way, a strong link between supply (capacity) and demand is maintained.

Streamlining production through process redesign

The second strategic measure introduced was a determined effort to improve process management at the NFI. As mentioned above, the Lean Six Sigma methodology was borrowed from industry and applied to eliminate waste of various kinds, including lost hours in the production processes. This made it possible to identify the variables that are critical to achieving the required speed and quality. Based on insights from this methodology, the NFI redesigned its processes, eliminating waiting time and economizing wherever possible to promote efficiency and speed.

The first step was to redesign processes to reduce "dead time"—*i.e.,* time that a case spends at the NFI but during which it is not being processed in any way. Rigorous analysis of every group at the NFI showed that the time spent conducting investigations was only a fraction of total delivery time. Throughout the remaining period, the investigation was simply in a state of suspended animation, waiting for the next step in the process to begin.

At first, there was some pushback to the effort to redesign the production processes at the NFI. Some professionals tend to distrust or even resent the idea of process management. Motivated by their profession and the content of their work, they fear that shortening delivery times will have a negative effect on quality. However, as the primary focus was on eliminating "dead time", no credible argument could be made that process redesign would have a negative effect on quality. And in fact, no such effect was observed.

Another concern was that process redesign would turn highly qualified employees into "assets" on a production line, who would carry out a limited set of standard tasks. In some cases, this may be a result of process redesign—especially when standardization is the solution to a particular problem. The current culture in many laboratories of journeymen forensic scientists involves taking cases sequentially "from crime scene all the way to the courtroom". In many cases this model is highly inefficient and unnecessary. Often the efficiency and throughput can be increased markedly by introducing a division of labor and some type of "assembly line" operations. Not all processes can be restructured in this way, but many can. Some forensic scientists may be concerned that a division of labor will make their work less interesting, or that they will not be able to control the (quality of the) whole process personally. The claim that quality necessarily suffers from this type of process redesign is unjustified. Nonetheless, a division of labor does have an impact on the way people work and on the content of their work. In some cases, job descriptions need to be reconciled with the appropriate level of education and qualifications required for the new jobs. Ph.D.'s are not required for conducting some of the jobs with highly standardized or repetitive tasks. Failure to redesign the processes could result in failure to achieve the appropriate efficiencies, which is not a realistic option in the long run, but failure to redefine the job descriptions could demoralize highly qualified forensic scientists because of a mismatch between expectations and requirements.

Refocusing R&D

The third strategic measure taken by the NFI to combat backlogs and long delivery times was to refocus its R&D efforts on finding innovative ways of increasing the speed of forensic processes. The NFI examined its own activities in R&D and concluded that these activities lacked a clear focus. Even though delivery times were the main concern of the customers, almost none of the R&D projects in the organization were aimed at creating technologies or methods to shorten them. Clearly, this had to change.

Looking at the whole range of R&D activities relating to forensics, three main categories could be discerned: basic research, applied research and product development. From the NFI's point of view, it was considered that basic research activities were best pursued in cooperation with universities and other partners, or left to them entirely. The NFI has been instrumental in setting up such a pure research program in The Netherlands, funded by the national science foundation (NWO).[6] Furthermore, we believe that improvement of the scientific underpinning and objectivity of forensic investigations would clearly benefit from a larger-scale, international effort. For this reason, the NFI has been seeking partners abroad, particularly in Europe and the United States.

The type of R&D that could most fruitfully be pursued by the NFI and other forensic service providers was the development of products and services, as this would fit in well with its chosen focus on customer needs. To guide innovation in this area, the NFI adopted the concepts of "Co-creation" and "Lean Innovation." These methods stress intensive cooperation and interaction between customer and provider in the innovation process. In this way, the R&D process is steered towards the innovations with the highest value for the customer. An example of a service that the NFI developed in this way was "DNA 6 hours." Inspired by the customer's need for speed in the delivery of results, this methodology guarantees that the customer receives a report on a crime scene DNA sample, including the results of a comparison with the DNA database, within 6 hours. In practice, however, the turnaround time is generally much shorter, at approximately 3.5 hours. Taking this idea further, the NFI has also introduced a "sprint portfolio": a set of very fast versions of the usual services provided by the NFI.

Results

Implementation of these three strategic measures has resulted in the elimination of the 2007 backlog of 18,000 cases (approximately 70,000 forensic investigations) and a remarkable decline in the average delivery time at the NFI. In 2007, average delivery time was approximately 140 days. This includes both "routine" investigations as well as highly complicated customized and interdisciplinary investigations. At the end of 2012, this number had fallen to 13.8 days, and it is still falling. This represents a reduction of the delivery time of more than 90 percent. Furthermore, "customer satisfaction" (which is measured every two years by an independent agency) has increased markedly, and is now at the same level as customer satisfaction at private companies in other sectors.

3. Defragmentation

Because of the relatively recent origins of forensic science and the institutional structure in which it arose, the field is fragmented. It is fragmented in the sense that it consists of dozens of different areas of expertise that rarely engage in deep interdisciplinary cooperation. The focus tends to be on areas of expertise, and on experts, rather than on providing integrated information services to customers. Furthermore, the field of forensic science is also fragmented because most forensic laboratories only serve the geographical jurisdiction of their main customer. In most cases, they only have one or two customers (*e.g.*, the local police force or prosecutor's office), which is partly caused by the fact that forensic labs in many cases are part of the main customer they serve. As a result, the field of forensics has developed into a sector comprising a large number of relatively small and local laboratories that necessarily act as pure production units. As an example, in the United States, much as in Europe, we find over 400 publicly funded forensic labs employing around 13,000 employees. Forensics still is a rather local affair. This is changing however.

No intrinsic borders

Forensic science and services are not intrinsically bound by jurisdictions or even national borders. In principle, therefore, there is nothing to prevent consolidation, collaboration, and cross-jurisdictional or even cross-border traffic of technology and services. Today, the fragmented condition of the forensic science sector remains

[6] NWO is the Netherlands Organization for Scientific Research

largely intact, but as the field continues to grow and innovate, it is inevitable that some forensic service providers will develop their own specialist capabilities, creating an irresistible stimulus for cross-jurisdictional traffic in forensic products and services. It would be unrealistic to assume that all local forensic laboratories, especially the smaller ones, would be able to provide state-of-the-art services across the full range of disciplines. Furthermore, they cannot be expected to have sufficient critical mass to ensure continuity and quality, or sufficient resources to support proprietary R&D programs. The reality is that most of them will remain pure production units in a limited number of forensic disciplines, containing small and vulnerable expert groups depending on just a few key people. Also, budgetary constraints, especially in an economic downturn such as we are experiencing now, will continue to put pressure on the forensic sector to produce more efficiently. Fragmentation costs money, because it cannot capture economies of scale and leads to suboptimal allocation and exploitation of what is essentially a very scarce resource.

More generally, the relatively small size of many laboratories, combined with the fact that they usually serve only one jurisdiction and operate solely within the criminal justice system, constitutes a significant and unnecessary impediment to the development of the field as a whole. This is true in relation to scientific knowledge and technology, and in relation to operational efficiency. For example, investments in equipment or R&D that may not make sense on a local level—because of insufficient caseload—may be justifiable on a regional or even global level. Similarly, such investments may make even more sense if the forensic laboratory is allowed to broaden its customer base, thus expanding the caseload still further and creating critical mass. Inevitably, setting up a modern forensic laboratory is an expensive business, due in part to the infrastructure required. Some disciplines are more expensive than others, but where, in particular, the fixed costs are high, significant economies of scale can be achieved as the size of the caseload increases. In other words, the fragmentation into many relatively small production units is inefficient, leads to vulnerabilities, contributes to the backlog problem, and is an obstacle to the kind of research and innovation that would propel the field forward.

Capacity problems

As stated above, forensic science is not a unified field, but rather a collection of specialist disciplines. At the NFI, for instance, more than 30 separate disciplines exist. Some of them are staffed by just a few experts, as the caseload is not large enough to justify additional staff. Consider just such a small discipline, staffed by three qualified forensic examiners. If one of them falls ill, attends a training course or leaves the organization, this will have a considerable impact on available capacity. Although such fluctuations in themselves pose considerable organizational problems and contribute to the growth of backlogs, the trouble they cause is, of course, compounded by the inevitable and unpredictable fluctuations in the inflow of cases. In addition, suppose the organization wishes to spend about 10 percent of its capacity on R&D in this field. In a team of three examiners, this amounts to 0.3 full-time equivalents: in other words, these examiners, either jointly or individually, can at best devote only a small portion of their work time to innovation. However, in the real world, the caseload is such that it will tend to drown out the R&D, with the result that no significant R&D effort is achieved at all. The result is stagnation of the field.

If the forensic laboratory could service a much larger geographical area and a larger number of customers, then the caseload at a certain point would become sufficient to support a staff with critical mass. If there are 10 or 20 qualified forensic examiners in the discipline in question, for instance, one or two of them could be freed up to conduct research full-time. Furthermore, a larger staff has much more flexibility to deal with setbacks such as illness. In short, the current fragmentation of the forensics sector, with its many, relatively small, laboratories, is not conducive to R&D, and gives rise to problems relating to flexibility and continuity.

Some might argue that the lack of R&D could be solved by creating a centralized system of R&D-oriented institutes, possibly at universities or other institutions. These would then perform most of the research. The theory is that this research would subsequently diffuse into the forensic system. There are reasons why a certain amount of skepticism towards this approach is justified. Experience shows that a severe disconnect is likely to arise between the central research institutes and the hundreds of production units doing all the casework. After all, even integrated technology companies find it a struggle to maintain an R&D program that accurately and continuously reflects their customers' needs. If (independent) research institutes are so far removed from actual casework and from customers, it will be very difficult to keep them on the right track. The probable outcome would be research that is very clever, but not necessarily what customers want or need. Customer needs are often surprising, as the NFI (and many companies in the private sector) have learned the hard way. In order to be able to appreciate customers' needs, it is necessary to remain in close contact with them and/or with those who will use the information provided by the investigations in question.

The foregoing suggests that it is forensic institutes themselves that are best placed to carry out R&D programs, alone or with partners. This, at least, provides some guarantee that results will be of the highest value to customers. However, in order for the institutes to be able to support significant R&D programs, to guarantee continuity and to capitalize on economies of scale, they need to create critical mass. This can be achieved by consolidation (fewer and larger institutions), by specialization, or by broadening their customer base to cover all government agencies that have a forensic need.

4. A growing need for training and education

As mentioned above, forensic investigations are becoming increasingly important and "mission critical" to customers. At the same time, forensic science and technology are becoming more complicated and difficult to understand for the layman. This constitutes one of the fundamental challenges of the field. For almost everyone, a suspect's confession is much easier to understand than, for example, the evidential value of a complex chemical analysis. Nevertheless, the latter may provide a much higher evidential value. Furthermore, using forensic investigations correctly, in a non-biased way, and interpreting results as intended, is not as easy as it may seem.

All this points to a growing need for training and education. This applies not only to forensic investigators, but even more so to the users of forensic information. This is largely due to a change in the whole process of criminal investigation. In a sense, the role forensics plays is similar to automation in factories: it "technologizes" the production process in criminal investigations. In manufacturing, the nature of the "human factor" has changed. Manual labor has been partially replaced by technology (machines) and knowledge workers (who design, create, and program the machines). Similarly, traditional labor-intensive investigative methods are being replaced or complemented by forensic science and technology. But this means that all the stakeholders in this process need to be trained to deal with this new situation. Police officers, prosecutors, and judges, for instance, need to know how to use forensics properly: they need to ask the right questions, and they need to interpret forensic results correctly.

Several years ago, in line with the need for more education and training, the NFI set up its own Academy with the express purpose of providing a wide range of stakeholders with the forensic knowledge and skills they need for their work. These stakeholders include forensic investigators, judges, police officers, first-responders, policy makers, and lawyers. Although each group has different requirements, the general aim is to train them to collect traces correctly (and not destroy important traces), to use forensic laboratories effectively (and ask the right questions), and to interpret the results of forensic investigations correctly. The NFI Academy has been a huge success, providing approximately 10,000 person-days of training in 2012 for interested practitioners from around the world.

5. An integrated model

Over the past few years, the NFI has implemented (and indeed is still implementing) an "integrated" organization model based on the analysis and principles presented above. This means that the organization not only provides forensic services to (domestic and foreign) government agencies, but that it also performs its own research and development in order to improve its services and create innovative new ones. In its R&D effort, the NFI cooperates with many companies, universities, and knowledge institutes around the world, especially in the Netherlands, Japan, and the United States. The R&D is partially financed by the fee received from customers who pay for the services of the NFI. The fact that the NFI can and does deliver products and services to government agencies in the Netherlands and abroad, as well as to intergovernmental organizations, is also part of the integrated model.

Forensic products and tools

The NFI still conducts many standardized "commodity" services. The organization also takes on a large and growing amount of custom work. This type of work often leads to specialized high-end products and tools, because examiners need them to do their cases. This may take the form of both hardware and software. Subsequently, such products and tools can be made available to the forensic community at large, to beneficial effect. However, the benefit goes beyond the immediate use of the product or tool. The revenues so earned are invested in new R&D to enhance current forensic capabilities and investigation techniques. If many integrated forensic institutes around the world were to do the same, this would create a whole new dynamic in the field. Conversely, if innovative products and tools that require large investments in R&D were distributed free of charge, this would only mean that funds to fuel the innovation engine would become depleted, stopping further innovation in its tracks. Laboratories that do not invest in R&D would benefit from the investments of others, who would subsequently become starved of funds themselves. Clearly, that is not a sustainable model for innovation, and it would perpetuate the situation in which most forensic laboratories are mere production units.

Concluding remarks

Forensic science is clearly at an important stage in its development. New advances in technology have placed forensics in an accelerating cycle of growth, as a wider range of parties than ever before comes to realize just how useful forensics can be for their own purposes. But this popularity—gratifying as it may be—nonetheless brings its own challenges, as laboratories become bogged down in work and customers become more demanding. This paper has reviewed some of the practical problems that the sector will need to resolve if it is to meet the demands of society: understanding what customers need, increasing the value of the information we provide to them, and generally accelerating our operations. More profoundly, however, we will need to undergo a shift in mindset and governance.

Several years ago, the NFI saw itself faced with these challenges and, in response, developed and implemented a number of measures that have enabled it to eliminate its backlogs and dramatically improve the quality and delivery times of its forensic investigations. In this way, it has been able to markedly improve customer satisfaction and has shown that its integrated model is a viable way forward. The forensic sector has great potential, but it will certainly find itself challenged to live up to the high expectations that customers and society have of it. It is equally certain that the sector can only succeed if it takes up the challenge and makes fundamental changes where necessary.

Acknowledgement

The author would like to thank Mr. Mark Stolorow (NIST, USA), Prof. Arian van Asten (NFI) and Mr. Marcel van der Steen (NFI) for their valuable contribution.

The CHAIRMAN. Thank you very much, sir.

Mr. Michael Bromwich?

STATEMENT OF MICHAEL R. BROMWICH, MANAGING PRINCIPAL, THE BROMWICH GROUP LLC AND PARTNER, GORDON PROCTER LLP

Mr. BROMWICH. Thank you very much, Chairman Rockefeller, Senator Thune, Senator Chiesa. I appreciate the opportunity to be here today.

Forensic science is a pivotal part of the criminal justice system on the Federal, state, and local level. It has the ability to identify suspects. It plays a significant role in a wide range of criminal cases. And as we have seen repeatedly over the past 20 years, it has the power to exonerate the innocent.

My background and experience with forensic science over the past 30 years has been as a prosecutor, defense lawyer, and investigative agency head, and through extensive investigations I have conducted of two important forensic labs. For the purposes of this brief statement, let me highlight the most relevant matters.

In 1994, I was serving as the Inspector General in the Department of Justice when we conducted an investigation of the FBI Lab. The investigation reviewed cases handled by three sections within the lab involved in analyzing bombing and explosives cases, including some of the most significant bombing and explosives cases handled in the previous decade. These included the World Trade Center bombing case in 1993 and the Oklahoma City bombing case in 1995.

The findings and conclusions of the investigation were stunning to forensic scientists in this country and abroad. The FBI Lab had long been viewed as the gold standard in forensic science and had exercised enormous worldwide influence on forensic labs. But our investigation found major flaws with many of the most significant cases we reviewed, including the World Trade Center and Oklahoma City bombing cases.

We found that analysts had performed work that lacked scientific rigor, reached unsupported conclusions, and in many cases were biased in favor of the prosecution. We recommended that many of the senior analysts and supervisors be removed from the lab, and we made broad institutional recommendations focusing on issues that included accreditation, report writing, standards development, and training.

In 2005, I was hired by the City of Houston to conduct an independent investigation of that city's police crime lab. For several years, the crime lab had been the subject of numerous allegations claiming that the work it performed was unscientific, inaccurate, and unreliable. We assembled a top-flight team of forensic scientists from throughout North America, and we reviewed more than 3,500 individual cases, making it the broadest review of a forensic science lab ever performed.

We found that many of the sections of the lab performed capable and reliable work, but we also found profound problems with the work the lab had performed in DNA and serology, with unacceptably high error rates in both areas. This was especially disturbing because DNA and serology analysis are conducted in the most serious cases, including homicides and sexual assaults. The errors in these cases had tragic human costs. They resulted in at least two highly publicized sexual assault cases in which innocent men were being sent to prison for crimes that they did not commit.

We found the problems in the HPD crime lab to be the result of many contributing factors, including lack of resources and support, poor management, insufficient quality control, inadequate training, inadequate protocols, lax supervision, and an insular culture.

Now, these two in-depth investigations were really threads in the broader fabric of concerns that were emerging in the 1990s and 2000s about the state of forensic science in this country. Forensic science disciplines that were at one time unquestioned were subjected to heightened scrutiny. Through the work of the Innocence Project and others, we learned of the enormous power of DNA analysis to exonerate defendants previously convicted of crimes.

The dark side of that equation was that, at the same time, we came to learn that non-DNA forensic analysis and testimony had frequently led to convictions based on excessive and unsupported claims about the strength and power of their conclusions. One study of DNA exonerations has shown that flawed forensic evidence contributed to approximately 50 percent of wrongful convictions overturned by DNA testing.

Now, the growing disquiet with the state of forensic science led to the 2005 congressional mandate to the National Academy of Sciences to conduct its study on the current state of forensic science, which was published in 2009. That carefully crafted report has become the touchstone for subsequent discussion of how best to reform the practice of forensic science.

In your letter inviting me to testify, you asked me to address the scope of the problems that can arise in crime labs and how improved standards, increased training, and accreditation might help to solve these problems. I have alluded to many of these in my summaries of our FBI and HPD lab investigation findings, and I have provided a more detailed list in my prepared statement.

We need to be realistic about the limitations of reform but also of its promise. Individual, nonsystemic errors by individual examiners can never be eliminated. Lab examiners are human, and they will make mistakes.

But sustained efforts to improve crime labs are possible and desirable through broad-based fundamental research into the scientific foundations of various disciplines, the creation of more uniform standards based on sound science, funding for more and better training, and developing meaningful systems of accreditation. These steps would raise the quality of the forensic science services provided throughout the Nation and diminish the number of errors.

The legislation introduced last session by Chairman Rockefeller, which focused on promoting research, requiring standards development, and implementing uniform standards, would be an enormous step in the right direction.

Finally, we have come a long way since the days not so very long ago when prosecutors, defense lawyers, and judges blindly accepted the findings and conclusions of crime lab analysts. Over the past 20 years, we have become all too familiar with their fallibility and the tragic consequences when their conclusions are flawed and their certainty is unjustified.

We have come to realize the shortcomings in the way forensic science is practiced in this country and the need for broad institutional reform. The challenge before us is to make a serious and sustained effort to address those deficiencies and improve the quality of justice provided in our criminal justice system. The people of this country deserve nothing less.

Thank you very much for your attention, and I, too, am happy to answer questions.

[The prepared statement of Mr. Bromwich follows:]

PREPARED STATEMENT OF MICHAEL R. BROMWICH, MANAGING PRINCIPAL, THE BROMWICH GROUP LLC AND PARTNER, GOODWIN PROCTER LLP

Mr. Chairman and Members of the Committee,

I appreciate the opportunity to be here today to provide my perspective on issues relating to strengthening forensic science in the United States. Forensic science is a pivotal part of the criminal justice system on the federal, state, and local level. Forensic science has the power to advance criminal investigations by helping to identify and exclude suspects, plays a significant role in the adversary system through expert reports and trial testimony, and, as we have seen repeatedly over the past 20 years, has the power to exonerate the innocent.

Let me share with you my background and experiences with forensic science, both as a participant in the criminal justice system over the last 30 years as a prosecutor, defense lawyer, and agency head, and through extensive investigations I have conducted of two important forensic labs.

From 1983 through 1989, I was a Federal prosecutor in New York and Washington, DC. My experience with forensic science and its techniques during that period was fairly typical for a prosecutor in the era that preceded the use of DNA. I worked with forensic scientists and analysts who provided reports and testimony on fingerprints, serology, controlled substances, and handwriting comparisons. With the exception of handwriting analysis, which was generally understood to be more subjective and less scientifically rigorous than the other fields, there was no controversy surrounding the forensic science reports that were produced or the courtroom testimony the analysts provided. They were accepted as true and beyond question.

Prosecutors happily embraced the boost that forensic science gave to their cases and did not question the analysis or the conclusions of the forensic examiners. Neither did defense counsel. These forms of forensic evidence were routinely admitted into evidence without challenge or controversy. In my seven years as a Federal prosecutor, I never heard any doubts expressed about the validity of the science underlying the reports and testimony used by my colleagues and me, nor did I ever see any instance of forensic evidence effectively challenged or excluded from evidence. In fact, I once secured convictions in a narcotics case after the drugs had been stolen from the prosecutor's office. The testimony of the chemist was enough.

In 1994, I was serving as the Inspector General of the Department of Justice (DOJ) when we began an investigation of the FBI Laboratory. Initially, the investigation focused on claims made by an FBI Lab scientist that one of his fellow examiners had altered analytic reports. After some of the initial allegations were substantiated, the investigation expanded to include a far broader review of cases handled by three sections within the FBI Lab that were involved in analyzing bombing and explosives cases. Eventually, the investigation came to include some of the most significant bombing and explosives cases handled by the FBI Lab in the previous decade, including the first World Trade Center bombing case (1993), the Oklahoma City bombing case (1995), the Avianca bombing case (1989), and many others. The Office of the Inspector General (OIG) report of investigation, published in April 1997, is available at: *http://www.justice.gov/oig/special/9704a/index.htm.*

The findings and conclusions of the investigation were stunning to forensic scientists in this country and abroad, and to officials in Federal and local law enforcement. The FBI Lab had long been viewed as the gold standard in forensic science, and had exercised enormous influence on forensic labs in the United States and around the world. Our investigation found major flaws and deficiencies with many of the most significant cases we reviewed, including the World Trade Center and Oklahoma City bombing cases. We found that many of the most senior analysts and supervisors in the FBI Lab had performed work that lacked scientific rigor, reached unsupported conclusions, and, in many cases, were biased in favor of the prosecution. We recommended that many of the senior analysts and supervisors be removed from the Lab because they had shown themselves to be unable or unwilling to conduct rigorous forensic analysis. We issued a set of broad institutional recommendations focusing on accreditation, organizational restructuring, report writing, quality assurance, documentation, the development of written protocols, and training.

The FBI reacted immediately to our broad set of 40 recommendations. When we returned a year later, we found that the FBI had done a responsible job of implementing those recommendations. Unfortunately, the same cannot be said of the efforts of a DOJ task force created to follow up on a large number of cases called into question by the OIG investigation. The operations of the DOJ task force were plagued by delays, lack of transparency, and the failure to notify defense lawyers representing clients in cases in which problematic forensic work was identified. The deficiencies in the work of the DOJ task force were highlighted in a series of stories published last year in the *Washington Post.*[1] In response, the DOJ Inspector General has launched an inquiry into the causes of those shortcomings.

In 2005, I was hired by the City of Houston to conduct an independent investigation of the Houston Police Department (HPD) Crime Lab. For several years, starting in 2002, the HPD Crime Lab had been the subject of numerous allegations claiming that the work it performed was unscientific, inaccurate, and unreliable. Those allegations encompassed virtually every section of the Lab, including DNA, serology, controlled substances, toxicology, trace evidence, firearms, and handwriting. The City attempted in various ways to address the problems in the Lab by bringing in consultants and a new Lab director, but continued public criticism of the Lab caused the HPD Chief of Police, with the blessing of the mayor, to seek an outside, independent review. To conduct the investigation, we assembled a top-flight team of forensic scientists from throughout North America. The team reviewed and analyzed cases in every forensic science discipline in which the Lab performed work. By the

[1] *http://www.washingtonpost.com/local/crime/doj-review-of-flawed-fbi-forensics-processes-lacked-transparency/2012/04/17/gIQAFegIPT_story.html; http://www.washingtonpost.com/local/crime/convicted-defendants-left-uninformed-of-forensic-flaws-found-by-justice-dept/2012/04/16/gIQAWTcgMT_story.html*

end of the investigation, we had reviewed more than 3,500 individual cases, making it the broadest review of a forensic science lab ever performed.

We found that many sections of the Lab performed capable and reliable work, but we also found profound problems with the work the Lab had performed in DNA and serology, with unacceptably high error rates in both areas of analysis. This was especially disturbing because DNA analysis and serology analysis are conducted in the most serious cases, including homicides and sexual assaults. We were so alarmed by the error rates we found in serology cases that we expanded our review to include a larger and broader set of cases than originally contemplated, reaching back to the 1980s. The errors in these DNA and serology cases were not without tragic human costs; they resulted, in at least two highly publicized sexual assault cases, with innocent men being sent to prison for crimes that subsequent analysis demonstrated that they could not have committed. We found the problems in the HPD Crime Lab to be the result of many factors, including lack of resources and support, poor management, insufficient quality control, inadequate training, inadequate protocols, lax supervision, and an insular culture in which Lab management for decades had prevented any meaningful external reviews. The reports issued in connection with that investigation are available at: *www.hpdlabinvestigation.org.*

These two in-depth investigations were threads in the broader fabric of concerns that were emerging in the 1990s and 2000s about the state of forensic science in this country. Forensic science disciplines that were at one time unquestioned came to be subjected to heightened scrutiny. Through the work of the Innocence Project and others, we learned of the enormous power of DNA analysis to exonerate defendants previously convicted of serious crimes. The dark side of that equation was that, at the same time, we came to learn that non-DNA forensic analysis and testimony had frequently led to convictions based on excessive and unsupported claims about the strength and power of their findings and conclusions. Indeed, flawed forensic science was in many instances revealed to be a key ingredient in securing wrongful convictions. One study of DNA exonerations has shown that flawed forensic evidence contributed to approximately 50 percent of wrongful convictions overturned by DNA testing.[2]

This growing disquiet with the state of forensic science led to the 2005 congressional mandate to the National Academy of Sciences (NAS) to conduct a study on the current state of forensic science in the United States, and ultimately to the 2009 publication of *Strengthening Forensic Science in the United States: A Path Forward.* That carefully crafted report has become the touchstone for subsequent discussion of how best to reform the practice of forensic science in this country. The report summarized its core finding in this way:

> The forensic science system, encompassing both research and practice, has serious problems that can only be addressed by a national commitment to overhaul the current structure that supports the forensic science community in this country. This can only be done with effective leadership at the highest levels of both Federal and state governments, pursuant to national standards, and with a significant infusion of Federal funds.

The recent activities of this Committee and the Senate Judiciary Committee are designed to help fully realize the promise of forensic science and to reduce the flaws and shortcomings that currently exist in the system. That promise is to focus investigations on legitimate suspects, aid in identifying and convicting the guilty, and help to exonerate the innocent. But our experience with the criminal justice system suggests that this bright promise cannot be achieved without the Federal leadership and funding called for by the NAS report.

In your letter inviting me to testify today, you asked me to address the scope of the problems that can arise in crime labs and how improved standards, increased training, and accreditation might help to solve these problems. Let me do so briefly. In the crime lab investigations I have conducted, the problems we discovered included the following:

- Individual, non-systemic errors made by individual lab examiners;
- Systemic errors made by groups of lab examiners due to lack of adequate training;
- Failures in supervision;
- Inadequate systems to ensure quality assurance and quality control;

[2] Brandon Garrett and Peter Neufeld, Virginia Law Review, Vol. 95, No. 1, March 2009, p. 8.

- Development and application of untested and unvalidated forensic procedures that are unique to individual examiners or groups of examiners and have not been peer reviewed;
- Outright fraud by examiners who have falsified analytic results;
- Skewing of analytic results in favor of the prosecution;
- Inadequate efforts to develop a culture of science within crime labs, including through staffing top leadership positions with qualified scientists;
- Failures of leadership at intermediate and top management levels in crime labs; and
- Absence of accreditation and other external reviews.

This is an extensive catalog of problems and issues, not all of which are susceptible to improvement in programs designed to address standards, training, and accreditation.

We need to be realistic about the limitations of reform but also of its potential to improve the quality of forensic science services delivered in this country. Individual, non-systemic errors by individual examiners can never be eliminated—lab examiners are human and they will make mistakes. But sustained efforts to improve crime labs are possible and desirable through 1) broad-based, fundamental research into the scientific foundations of various forensic disciplines; 2) the creation of more uniform standards based on sound science; 3) funding more and better training; and 4) developing meaningful systems of accreditation. These steps would undoubtedly raise the quality of the forensic science services provided throughout the Nation and diminish the number of errors.

In my investigations of the two major crime labs, my teams found that deficiencies in standards, training, and the absence of accreditation played major roles in the problems we examined.

- In the investigation of the FBI Lab, the team found that:
  - "Meaningful peer review and reliance on validated procedures would have prevented" many of the flawed conclusions reached by FBI Lab analysts;
  - There was no coordinated, overall training program within the Lab; and
  - Until 1994, there had been no effort by the FBI to seek accreditation or other types of external reviews.
- In the investigation of the HPD Crime Lab, the team found that
  - Standard Operating Procedures consisted of materials cobbled together over time without adequate reevaluation and reorganization, and virtually no technical reviews of analysts' work;
  - The majority of errors found in the Lab's work were the product of poor training and lack of competent technical guidance and supervision rather than intentional misconduct; and
  - Lab management failed to make meaningful efforts to seek accreditation from recognized outside bodies.

If these two labs were isolated instances of the problems created by inadequate standards, poor training, and lack of accreditation, there might not be a need for a broad, national solution. But the NAS report concluded, after a lengthy and detailed review, that these problems are pervasive. I agree.

The legislation introduced last session by Chairman Rockefeller, which focused on promoting research, requiring standards development, and implementing uniform standards, would be an enormous step in the right direction. In view of the central importance that the various forensic sciences play in our criminal justice system, the lack of funding for basic and applied research in forensic science cannot be defended. The bill called for the development of a national forensic science research strategy developed by the National Science Foundation, a forensic science grant program, and the creation of forensic science research centers. In addition, it called for the National Institute of Standards and Technology (NIST) to develop forensic science standards, in consultation with standards development organizations and other stakeholders, including current participants in the forensic science system. Finally, it called for the formation of a Forensic Science Advisory Committee cochaired by the Director of NIST and the Attorney General.

The Justice Department has already taken one step in the right direction. As you know, in February 2013, the Attorney General published a Federal Register Notice announcing the formation of the National Commission on Forensic Science. The Commission's responsibilities will include recommending strategies for enhancing quality assurance in forensic science units. Its duties will include:

- Recommending priorities for standards development;
- Reviewing forensic science subject matter guidance developed by subject matter experts;
- Developing proposed guidance relating to the use of forensic science in the criminal justice system;
- Developing policy recommendations, including:
  - A uniform code of professional responsibility; and
  - Minimum requirements for training, accreditation and/or certification; and
- Identifying the current and future requirements to strengthen forensic science and meet growing demand.

The membership of the National Commission has not yet been determined. Whether it is capable of realizing the ambitions of the Notice announcing its formation remains to be seen, but DOJ should be applauded for taking the first major institutional step in the direction of providing high-level Federal attention to some of the most important issues implicating the delivery of forensic science services.

The formation of the National Commission is an important step, but much more needs to be done. It does not eliminate the need for achieving the other goals contained in the legislation proposed last year. The imperatives of basic and applied research remain undiminished, as does the need for focused efforts on developing and refining standards for forensic science. As the NAS report concluded, "although congressional action will not remedy all of the deficiencies in forensic science methods and practices, truly meaningful advances will not come without significant concomitant leadership from the Federal Government."

We have come a long way since the days—not so very long ago—when prosecutors, defense lawyers, and judges blindly accepted the findings and conclusions of crime lab analysts. Over the past 20 years, we have become all too familiar with the fallibility of crime lab analysts and the tragic consequences when their conclusions are flawed and their certainty is unjustified. We have come to realize the shortcomings in the way forensic science is practiced in this country and the need for broad institutional reform. The challenge before us is to make a serious and sustained effort to address the deficiencies that have been identified and to improve the quality of justice provided throughout this country. The people of this country deserve nothing less.

Thank you for your attention. I am happy to answer any questions you may have.

The CHAIRMAN. Thank you, sir.

Dr. Gregory Schmunk, National Association of Medical Examiners, Chief Medical Examiner.

Please.

STATEMENT OF GREGORY A. SCHMUNK, M.D., PRESIDENT, NATIONAL ASSOCIATION OF MEDICAL EXAMINERS AND CHIEF MEDICAL EXAMINER, POLK COUNTY MEDICAL EXAMINER'S OFFICE

Dr. SCHMUNK. Chairman Rockefeller, Ranking Member Thune, Senator Chiesa, thank you very much for giving me the opportunity to speak today.

I am a board-certified forensic pathologist. I am also a registered diplomat with the American Board of Medicolegal Death Investigators. And I am representing the National Association of Medical Examiners, which is a professional society representing over 1,100 forensic pathologists, medical examiners, medico-legal death investigators, and coroners in the U.S.

Our organization has long been supportive of efforts to draft legislation for the death investigation community. In fact, as members of the Consortium of Forensic Science Organizations, we have long asked for legislation to be written creating a Federal structure that will provide guidance and leadership for our community.

I want to emphasize that my remarks today, however, will primarily focus on forensic pathology and death investigation and not on the crime labs.

NAME believes that it is critical to have national uniformity in death investigation policies, to ensure proper training and recruitment of forensic pathologists, to improve communication between medico-legal jurisdictions, and to create a mechanism for the proper distribution of death investigation data.

The report in 2009 contained many recommendations for improving the quality of forensic services, including medico-legal death investigation, in the United States. NAME has endorsed those recommendations of the council. We believe that there needs to be a formal and Federal entity which oversees death investigation. We believe that by having this entity we could address most of our major concerns and specifically ensure the issue of continuity and quality.

NAME does believe that the accreditation of offices and the certification of medical examiners, coroners, and death investigators should be mandatory. NAME has had professional practice standards for autopsy performance since 2005. Forensic pathologists have been board-certified by the American Board of Pathology since 1964. And the American Board of Medicolegal Death Investigations has certified medical death investigators since 2005. But many offices throughout this country are staffed by noncertified practitioners.

NAME has also had a professional system of medico-legal office accreditation in place since 1974. But, unfortunately, due to the lack of any Federal mandate for accreditation, only 70 out of 465 medico-legal death investigation offices are currently accredited in the United States, approximately one-third of the population.

So the standards exist, but we do not have the leadership and carrot-and-stick approach to enforce them within the medical examiner community. Since forensic pathologists receive very little Federal funding, it is difficult to enforce any such standards on the Federal level. We do receive Paul Coverdell Forensic Science Act funding, but that was not funded by the administration this year. And since its inception in 2000, Coverdell has been funded only five times.

Increased Federal funding of the forensic pathology programs could represent the carrot to encourage states to adopt uniform standards. Existing standards should not be phased out but should be a starting point and should grow with the science.

NAME has attempted to garner interest in drafting a new national model medical examiner legislation without success. The last law was in 1954, and it is obsolete. There are various death investigation systems throughout the country, including medical examiner, sheriff-coroner in California, district attorney coroner in Nebraska, and elected coroner.

A constituent from one of your states may die in his jurisdiction where the investigator is not trained in death investigation, operates under budget shortages, and uses no required guidelines. The office may not take jurisdiction of the case, may not request an autopsy, or may misinterpret the medical findings of the autopsy.

NAME strongly also feels that incentive funds should be provided to states and jurisdictions to ensure that death investigation systems in the country are all of uniform excellence. This could be done by providing support for accreditation and certification or by encouraging regionalizations.

The variable death investigation was an expose in "Frontline," NPR, and ProPublica in 2011.

But another problem we have is not enough forensic pathologists. There are an estimated 500 board-certified forensic pathologists in the United States and——

The CHAIRMAN. Excuse me, sir. Not enough what?

Dr. SCHMUNK. Forensic pathologists.

The CHAIRMAN. OK.

Dr. SCHMUNK. Approximately 500 currently practice in the United States. We need approximately 1,000, according to estimates. This is most pronounced in rural areas.

Only 30 to 40 forensic pathologists are graduated each year. As many of the programs that train forensic pathologists are not associated with medical schools where there is graduate funding for education, the funding for training is often from local tax dollars.

Until we achieve these points, we will not have systems that are run professionally in an accredited office with board-certified forensic pathologists.

A matter of great importance is communication among the states. There was a program, the Medical Examiner and Coroner Information Sharing Program, in the CDC in 1986, but that was funded out in 2004. We believe that this office should be recreated.

We also support the concept of basic and applied research in forensic science and forensic pathology in particular. Evidence-based medicine is a big thing for us, and that will improve the quality of forensic death investigation and ensuring the confidence in the outcomes.

I would like to thank you for the opportunity of speaking to you today, and I welcome any questions.

[The prepared statement of Dr. Schmunk follows:]

PREPARED STATEMENT OF GREGORY A. SCHMUNK, M.D., PRESIDENT, NATIONAL ASSOCIATION OF MEDICAL EXAMINERS AND CHIEF MEDICAL EXAMINER, POLK COUNTY MEDICAL EXAMINER'S OFFICE

Mr. Chairman, Ranking Member Thune, and Members of the Committee:

Thank you for giving me the opportunity to testify before you today regarding science and standards in forensics and specifically how those issues are reflected in the Medical Examiner community.

My name is Gregory Schmunk and I am a physician certified by the American Board of Pathology in Anatomic and Forensic Pathology and a Registered Diplomat with the American Board of Medicolegal Death Investigators (ABMDI). I am Chief Medical Examiner for Polk County, Iowa in the City of Des Moines. I am here today representing the National Association of Medical Examiners (NAME) as their President. NAME is the professional society representing over 1,100 Forensic Pathologists, Medical Examiners, Medicolegal Death Investigators, and Coroners in the United States.

My organization has long been supportive of the efforts to draft legislation for the Death Investigation community in both your Committee and the Judiciary Committee. In fact, as members of the Consortium of Forensic Science Organizations we have long asked for legislation to be written creating a Federal structure that will provide guidance and leadership for our community. We believe that it is critical to have national uniformity in death investigation policies, to ensure proper training and recruitment of trained pathologists to ensure the quality investigations, to improve the frequent lack of communication between medico-legal jurisdictions, and to create a mechanism for the proper distribution of death investigation data not only in the forensic community but also the public health, public safety, and homeland security communities.

In 2009, the National Research Council (NRC) published a report, *Strengthening Forensic Science in the United States: A Path Forward.*[1] This report contained many recommendations for improving the quality of forensic services including medico-legal death investigation in the United States. We believe many of those recommendations, if implemented, could resolve many of the problems within the Medical Examiner community. In July of 2009, NAME passed a resolution[2] strongly endorsing the recommendations of the Council and specifically endorsed the establishment of a National Institute of Forensic Sciences to promote the development of forensic science into a mature field of multidisciplinary research and practice based on scientific principles.

NAME has long believed that there needs to a formal and Federal entity which overseas forensic science and death investigation. We believe that by having this entity exist we could address most of our major concerns and specifically the continuity of quality. However, it is important to recognize that the entity must take into consideration the fact that a complete death investigation determines the cause of death and can thus assist in a criminal investigation.

NAME specifically endorsed the NRC recommendation that accreditation and individual certification of forensic science professionals, specifically medical examiners, should be mandatory. NAME has had professional practice standards for autopsy performance since 2005.[3] These standards are under constant review and revision. NAME has also had a professional system of medico-legal office accreditation in place since 1974[4] and is currently working towards ISO certification of our system. Unfortunately, due to the lack of any Federal or state mandates for accreditation, only 70 out of over 465[5] offices performing forensic autopsies are currently accredited in the United States. This is up from 40 offices in 2004. NAME accredited offices serve a total of just over 102 million persons or around ⅓ of the population. Forensic Pathologists have been individually certified by the American Board of Pathology[6] since 1964. The American Board of Medicolegal Death Investigators (ABMDI)[7] has certified Medicolegal Death Investigators since 2005. Unfortunately, additional certification bodies have risen with less rigorous certification standards.[8]

This clearly points to the fact that the standards exist but we lack the leadership and carrot/stick to enforce them within the medical examiner community. Since forensic pathologists receive very little Federal funding so it is difficult to enforce any such standards. In fact, the only funding we receive is that under the Paul Coverdell Forensic Science Act which was not funded by the Administration this year. Since its inception in 2000 Coverdell has been funded in the Federal budget less than five times. Increased Federal funding of forensic pathology programs could represent the "carrot" to encourage states to adopt uniform standards.

Therefore, no current Federal or uniform state standards exist for death investigation other than the voluntary NAME standards previously mentioned and the death investigation standards issued by the National Institutes of Justice in 1999.[9] We think it is important to point out here that we do not believe that these standards should be thrown out. Rather, we believe they are a starting point and should grow with the science. But as noted there is very little Federal funding that goes to our community that could enforce standards. To that end it is critical that grants be cre-

---

[1] *Strengthening Forensic Science in the United States: A Path Forward* accessed 6/23/2013 at *http://www.nap.edu/catalog.php?record_id=12589*

[2] National Association of Medical Examiners Executive Committee and Board of Directors Resolution on National Research Council (NRC) of the National Academies report "Strengthening Forensic Science in the United States: A Path Forward." July 2009

[3] NAME Autopsy Performance Standards 2013 accessed 6/23/2013 at *https://netforum.avectra.com/eweb/DynamicPage.aspx?Site=NAME&WebCode=PubIA*

[4] NAME Accreditation Checklist 2009–2014 accessed 6/23/2013 at *https://netforum.avectra.com/eweb/DynamicPage.aspx?Site=NAME&WebCode=PubIA*

[5] National Association of Medical Examiners, *Preliminary Report on America's Medicolegal Offices* (180 day report to the Senate Appropriations Committee; findings presented at the National Institute of Justice Summit on Forensic Sciences Services, May 2004) accessed 6/23/2013 at *http://www.nij.gov/nij/pubs-sum/213420.htm*

[6] *http://www.abpath.org/*

[7] *http://www.abmdi.org/*

[8] "No Forensic Background? No Problem" accessed 6/23/2013 at *http://www.propublica.org/article/no-forensic-background-no-problem*

[9] "Death Investigation: A Guide for the Scene Investigator—Technical Update", National Institutes of Justice 2011, accessed 6/23/2013 at *http://www.nij.gov/pubs-sum/234457.htm*

ated and funded based on the needs of the forensic community. There needs to be Federal guidance and leadership in mandating standards.

NAME has attempted to garner interest in drafting new national model medical examiner legislation without success. The last model legislation was issued in 1954 and is obsolete. Various death investigation systems exist around the country such as Medical Examiner, Sheriff-Coroner (California), District Attorney-Coroner (Nebraska), and elected Coroner. Thus a constituent from one of your states may be in a jurisdiction where the coroner is not trained in death investigation, operates under a budget shortage, and uses no required guidelines. They may not take jurisdiction of a case, not request an autopsy or misinterpret the medical findings of the autopsy. The 65 year old crash victim may not have visible injuries and be certified as a natural death or the decedent in the motel room may have a detectable and heritable cardiac condition which could have been found at autopsy, giving the surviving children opportunity to assess their own risks for a similar condition. Recently, an under-funded system in North Carolina missed rapid diagnosis of two carbon monoxide deaths in a motel room, resulting in a third death of a child.[10] The variability of death investigation and the effects on your constituents was the subject of an extensive exposé by NPR, Frontline, and ProPublica in 2011.[11]

But we must also make sure that we have enough pathologists in the country to perform the job. A recent report from the Justice Department[12] addressed workforce shortages and blames the shortage of forensic pathologists on limited numbers of training programs and low pay in relation to other medical subspecialties. An estimated 500 board certified forensic pathologists are currently in practice; it is estimated that at least 1,000 are needed to meet even the minimal needs of the country. The lack of board certified forensic pathologists is more pronounced in rural areas. An alarming trend is the lack of medical students pursuing a career in forensic pathology. While there are 131 medical schools in the U.S. only 37 forensic pathology training programs exist. Of the 77 approved training positions in 2012 only 52 were funded and only 42 were actually filled.[13] Of the 30–40 forensic pathologists trained each year some choose not to practice forensics and only two-thirds choose to practice full time. The supply is thus barely able to keep up with the attrition in the field due to death, retirement and decisions to move into a better compensated and less stressful branch of pathology. As many of these programs are not associated with medical schools (where funding for graduate medical education is sometimes available), funding for forensic pathology training often comes from local tax dollars, if at all.

NAME is strongly in agreement with the NRC recommendation that incentive funds should be provided to states and jurisdictions with the goal of ensuring that all death investigation systems in the country are of uniform excellence. Until this is achieved we will continue to see some parts of our country which have systems which are not run professionally, in an accredited Medical Examiner system, with all forensic autopsies performed or directly supervised by board certified forensic pathologists. We will continue to have a shortage of forensic pathologists and many forensic autopsies will be performed each day by individuals who are not trained in the profession, sometimes even by non-pathologists. The shortage of forensic pathologists has even led to physician extenders, such as autopsy assistants, performing medico-legal autopsies in some jurisdictions[14] and even testifying in homicide trials.[15] In fact, due to the lack of standards, death investigations are commonly performed in the country by individuals with no specific training (including either persons with no medical training or paramedics, nurses and EMTs).

Another matter of great importance to our community is that of communication and data sharing among States. Surprisingly this is another victim of the lack of leadership from the Federal Government in forensic science and medico-legal death

---

[10] "Failures in state medical examiner system were exposed, not fixed" accessed 6/23/2013 at *http://www.newsobserver.com/2013/06/22/2982968/failures-in-state-medical-examiner.html*

[11] "Medical Examiners In America: A Dysfunctional System" accessed 6/23/2013 at *http://www.huffingtonpost.com/2011/02/02/the-real-csi-how-americas_n_816842.html* and "Post Mortem: Death Investigation in America" accessed 6/23/2013 at *http://www.propublica.org/series/post-mortem*

[12] "PRC#5: Increasing the Supply of Forensic Pathologists in the United States: A Report and Recommendations" accessed 6/23/2013 at *http://swgmdi.org/index.php?option=com_content&view=article&id=90&Itemid=103*

[13] Report of Forensic Pathology Fellows in the United States 2011–12 Academic Year Prepared by Randy Hanzlick, MD, Chair, NAME ad hoc Data Committee

[14] "Was a Bachelor of Science performing unsupervised forensic autopsies in Missouri?" accessed 6/23/2013 at *http://pathologyblawg.com/?s=parcells*

[15] "Loughridge murder trial begins" accessed 6/23/2013 at *http://www.waynesvilledailyguide.com/article/20120911/NEWS/120919648#axzz2X4z7dIpN*

investigation. In 1986, he Medical Examiner/Coroner Information Sharing Program (MECISP) was established by the Centers for Disease Control and Prevention (CDC) because of the lack of uniformity in national death investigation policies, the frequent lack of communication between medico-legal jurisdictions, and the need for more wide-spread distribution of death investigation data. The primary goals of the MECISP were:

- To improve the quality of death investigations in the United States and to promote the use of more standardized policies for when and how to conduct these investigations.
- To facilitate communication among death investigators, the public health community, Federal agencies, and other interested groups.
- To improve the quality, completeness, management, and dissemination of information on investigated deaths.
- To promote the sharing and use of medical examiner and coroner (ME/C) death investigation data.

Unfortunately, due to changes in administrative policy in 2004 this office ceased to exist and with it went our ability to communicate and share data across borders. We believe this office needs to be recreated.

NAME endorses the position of the NRC report that support for basic and applied research in forensic science and forensic pathology in particular is needed. The application of evidence based medicine is essential to improving the quality of forensic death investigation and ensuring confidence in the outcomes. In addition, the provision of grants to state and county systems to improve the overall quality of forensic pathology services would serve to raise the bar for death investigation across the nation, allowing antiquated and inadequate systems to be replaced by modern medical examiner systems using certified practitioners in accredited offices. This could be accomplished, for example, by providing support for accreditation and certification or by encouraging regionalization in order to conserve scarce resources.

A major focus of the Federal Government is currently in health care. The Affordable Care Act, or any subsequent modifications to improve health care in the country, does have an ultimate focus on quality and accountability. Although possibly not directly within the scope of this committee, I would like to note that the national autopsy rate is miserably low at about 8.5 percent of deaths. The gold standard for healthcare accountability is the autopsy. Unfortunately when the Joint Commission on Accreditation of Healthcare Organizations dropped its requirement for a minimum hospital autopsy rate of 20 percent in the mid-1970s, hospitals across the country stopped doing autopsies, which are uncompensated by Medicare or any insurance program and are thus a drain on the bottom line. Medical Examiners and Coroners around the country have become the *de facto* autopsy service for the country. But with manpower issues and funding deficiencies, many autopsies which could provide essential information are left undone. Many studies have shown that the autopsy provides quality control to the medical community, in addition to the contribution to public health. As an example, trauma systems around the country regularly audit their provision of care by means of peer review. When a death has resulted from trauma, the autopsy plays a vital role in detecting injuries which may have been missed. This helps to allow trauma systems to evaluate whether a death may have been preventable. An autopsy may not be performed if sufficient medical information is available from hospitalization, even though the death lies within medical examiner jurisdiction. Thus, even though the legal obligation of the medical examiner system is fulfilled, valuable additional information of value to the medical and legal communities may be lost, often for simply fiscal reasons.

In conclusion, I would like to thank you for this opportunity to address the Committee today. I also thank you for what you have done thus far and we look forward to the continued discussion with you and your staff in order to achieve the much needed Federal leadership that we require in the field of forensics.

RESOLUTION

NATIONAL ASSOCIATION OF MEDICAL EXAMINERS

EXECUTIVE COMMITTEE

JULY 2, 2009

Be it resolved:

The National Association of Medical Examiners (NAME) strongly endorses all of the recommendations of the National Research Council (NRC) of the National Academies encompassed in the report "Strengthening Forensic Science in the United States: A Path Forward."

The NAME Executive Committee has the following specific comments on the recommendations:

Recommendation #1

The first and most important NAS recommendation is that a new and independent National Institute of Forensic Sciences (NIFS) be established to promote the development of forensic science into a mature field of multidisciplinary research and practice founded on the systematic collection and analysis of data. NAME strongly supports this recommendation and sees it as the foundation for the remainder of the NRC recommendations. NAME also recognizes that there might be impediments to establishing a new institute at this time. If NIFS is unattainable at present, NAME believes that the duties of this agency should be placed as a bridging step into a new Office of Forensic Services (OFS) within an existing agency fulfilling the spirit of the NRC recommendations.

The report outlines that one of the functions of NIFS is to establish and enforce best practices for forensic science professionals. In the arena of medico-legal death investigation, NAME has established forensic autopsy performance standards that can be used for this purpose.

NAME believes that an essential function of NIFS would be to conduct periodic forensic science needs assessments at the federal, state, regional, and local levels in order to ensure optimal provision of resources to service providers. Such assessments should also consider research needs. The assessment results should be presented in a report.

Recommendation #4

NAME supports the NRC recommendation that all public forensic science laboratories including medical examiner and coroner offices should be independent from or administratively autonomous within law enforcement agencies or prosecutor offices. Provisions should be made to assure the technical and professional autonomy of forensic service providers at all levels. The goal is to have unbiased professional testing and reporting and the absence of real and perceived conflicts of interest. We agree, that to achieve this end will require incentive funds as indicated in the report.

Recommendation #5

NAME endorses the recommendation that research programs on human observer bias and sources of human error in forensic examinations including studies to determine contextual bias in forensic practice should be encouraged. However, NAME urges caution in the arena of contextual information and forensic pathology. Medical examiners are physicians who operate in the medical paradigm of using a clinical history and information about the circumstances surrounding a death to generate hypotheses about potential causative diseases and injuries. The autopsy and laboratory examination allows a forensic pathologist to confirm or refute these hypotheses and reach medical conclusions. Autopsy is the practice of medicine. The history and circumstances provide the context for the autopsy and laboratory findings. In addition to determining cause of death, medical examiners are directed to determine the manner of death, which is largely based on the circumstances surrounding death.

Recommendation #7

NAME endorses the recommendation that laboratory accreditation and individual certification of forensic science professionals should be mandatory and all forensic science professionals should have access to a certification process. In the arena of medico-legal death investigation NAME believes that all death investigators should at least be certified by the American Board of Medicolegal Death Investigators at the registry (basic) level. All pathologists performing medico-legal autopsies should be certified by the American Board of Pathology in forensic pathology. All medico-legal death investigation offices and agencies should be accredited using professional consensus practice standards such as those developed by NAME. To achieve such ideals will require funding to improve the organization and operations of many medico-legal death investigation offices. Training programs and certifying and accrediting bodies will likely also need funding to process increasing numbers of applicants.

Recommendation #11

NAME fully supports the recommendation ideal that incentive funds should be provided to states and jurisdictions with the goal of replacing coroner systems with medical examiner systems. These funds should be used to build facilities, purchase necessary equipment, improve administration, and ensure education, training and staffing of offices. To foster this transition, NAME supports the recommendation that NIFS should work with the National Conference of Commissioners on Uniform State Laws, the American Law Institute and NAME to draft legislation for a modern model death investigation code. NAME also supports the recommendation that all medico-legal autopsies should be performed or directly supervised by a board certified (American Board of Pathology) forensic pathologist and that this standard should be phased in over a defined period of time. As a more immediate step, NAME believes it essential that all medico-legal death investigative systems incorporate the leadership of a board certified forensic pathologist. Efforts to achieve more uniformity in medico-legal death investigation can be hindered by the severe lack of resources (financial, personnel, equipment, and training) on a national level. Each of these resources should be addressed in order to improve our national medico-legal death investigation infrastructure on a jurisdictional or state level.

The report also recommends that NIFS and the National Institutes of Health (NIH) promote scholarly, competitive peer-reviewed research and technical development in forensic medicine and develop a strategy to improve forensic pathology research. This recommendation includes the provision of research funding and the development of a study section to establish research goals and evaluate research proposals. This goal is reinforced in recommendations #1 and 3. NAME enthusiastically supports these recommendations. Forensic pathology supports both public health and public safety but this combined role has often remained unrecognized. Historically, minimal research funds have been provided for forensic pathology research by the Centers for Disease Control and Prevention and the National Institute of Justice.

NAME also supports the recommendation that NIFS/NIH in conjunction with NAME and the American Board of Medicolegal Death Investigators establish a Scientific Working Group (SWG) for forensic pathology and medico-legal death investigation. NAME agrees that this committee should develop and promote standards for best practices, administration, staffing, education, training, and continuing education for competent death scene investigation and postmortem examinations. NAME believes that this committee should be led by and have strong representation from board certified forensic pathologists.

As also articulated in recommendation #7, NAME supports the concept that all medical examiner offices should be accredited pursuant to NIFS endorsed standards and believes that professional consensus accreditation standards such as those developed by NAME should become the NIFS standard. Restricting Federal funding to offices that are accredited or making measurable and significant progress towards accreditation is appropriate.

As outlined in the report, recruitment of qualified practitioners into the forensic pathology should be enhanced. NAME supports the recommendation that funding in the form of medical student loan forgiveness and/or fellowship support should be made available to pathology residents who choose forensic pathology as their specialty. Increasing the numbers of forensic pathologists will facilitate the transition from coroner to medical examiner systems.

Report of Forensic Pathology Fellows in the United States

2011–12 Academic Year

Prepared by Randy Hanzlick, MD, Chair, NAME ad hoc Data Committee

A few years back, here were about 40 ACGME-accredited forensic pathology training programs in the United States. In recent years, the number has been 37. IN the past year or so, two of those programs have become inactive (Newark NJ and Oklahoma City). Thus, there are technically 35 active forensic pathology fellowship training programs. Locations, number of ACGME-approved positions, number of funded positions, and number of filled positions is shown below.

Name of the Sponsoring Institution	Number of approved positions	Number of funded positions	Filled positions
Allegheny County	2	2	1
Armed Forces Medical Examiner	4	0	0
Bexar County Medical Examiner's Office	2	1	1
Broward County Medical Examiner's Office	2	1	1
Cook County Office of the Medical Examiner	2	1	1
Cuyahoga County Medical Examiner's Office	3	1	1
Emory University School of Medicine	2	1	1
Harris County	2	2	1
Hennepin County Medical Examiner	1	1	1
Indiana University	1	1	1
Jackson County Medical Examiner's Office	1	1	0
Los Angeles County Coroner	6	2	1
Massachusetts	4	2	0
Medical College of Wisconsin/Milwaukee County MEO	2	1	1
Medical University of South Carolina	1	1	1
Miami-Dade County Medical Examiner Department	4	4	4
Montgomery County Coroner's Office (Ohio)	1	0	0
New York City Office of Chief Medical Examiners	4	4	4
Office of the Chief Medical Examiner's—State of Maryland	4	3	3
Office of the Medical Examiner Metro Nashville/Davidson County	2	2	0
Puerto Rico	0	0	0
Saint Louis University	1	1	1
San Diego County Medical Examiner	2	1	1
Seattle-King County	2	1	0
Southwestern Institute of Forensic Sciences	3	2	2
Tarrant County Medical Examiner's District	1	1	1
UNC Hospitals	2	1	2
University of Alabama at Birmingham	1	1	0
University of Colorado Denver	1	1	1
University of Louisville	1	1	1
University of New Mexico	4	4	4
University of South Florida	2	1	1
VCU-Richmond	4	4	3
Wake Forest University School of Medicine	1	1	1
Wayne County Medical Examiner (Detroit)	2	1	1
TOTAL	77	52	42

Thus, only 68 percent of approved positions are funded, and 81 percent of the funded positions are filled with a total of 42 fellows this year. 8 of the 35 programs (23 percent) have no fellow this year.

The CHAIRMAN. Thank you, sir, very much.

Ms. Jill Spriggs, Secretary, Consortium of Forensic Science Organizations.

STATEMENT OF JILL SPRIGGS, SECRETARY, CONSORTIUM OF FORENSIC SCIENCE ORGANIZATIONS

Ms. SPRIGGS. Mr. Chairman, Ranking Member Thune, and members of the Committee, thank you for asking me to testify before this committee on matters of forensic science.

My name is Jill Spriggs, and I am the Crime Laboratory Director for the Office of the District Attorney, Sacramento County Laboratory of Forensic Services. I am also the past President of the American Society of Crime Laboratory Directors. In my career, I have overseen the daily operations of both a state and local crime laboratory, so I come from that unique perspective.

Today I am here representing the Consortium of Forensic Science Organizations, or CFSO, which represents over 12,000 forensic service providers.

As you know, the National Academies released in February 2009 a report on the state of forensic science in this nation. This report distills down to two operational and scientific needs: one, standardization in education, training, and forensic science delivery; two, resources across the forensic science community.

In fact, the forensic science provider community requested Federal legislation to provide guidance and leadership to our community in response to this report. And still, 4 years later, this has not happened. In the absence of legislation, the Executive Branch has taken numerous efforts to reshape forensic science, such as the creation of the National Commission on Forensic Science.

I would like to take this opportunity to lay out for this committee what we believe to be the greatest challenges facing the forensic community and solutions to solve them.

First, while we do believe the Federal Government should be involved in state and local forensic science to maintain consistency and guidance, we do not believe a Federal oversight organization should be created. While the work the crime laboratory performs is ultimately the same, differences among state jurisdictions need to be considered, and there is not a one-size-fits-all approach.

We believe and strongly support the creation of an office of forensic science in the Department of Justice to coordinate and lead on matters of accreditation, training, education, certification, and resource allocation.

Second, many seem to believe there currently exist no standards on training or education in forensic science. There are currently 22 scientific working groups, or SWGs, who build consensus standards in the specific forensic disciplines they represent, as well as training guidelines and improvement in practices in the disciplines themselves.

Federal, state, and local forensic scientists and other experts are represented on these SWGs, as well as academia, attorneys, judges, private laboratory scientists, and independent consultants. Historically, these SWGs have operated on very slim budgets and have succeeded in bringing to the forensic disciplines the much-needed structure.

Why is the administration budgeting a program to create working groups that many believe will undo the work of the SWGs? An inordinate amount of money to start over is being proposed in the 2014 Federal budget. CFSO supports NIST advising the SWG groups in order to give the SWGs the much-needed support, but to start over and reinvent the wheel is not needed and costly. This will prove extremely disruptive to the scientific community, as it waits for years for new standards to be disseminated and vetted.

Third, research is an absolutely critical part of how we advance our science, as forensic science is just that, a science. Research is critical, but it has to be in the context of the requirements of the forensic science community. What is needed in the forensic science community is applied science, and by that I mean science that is taken from basic research so it can be applied in the crime laboratory.

Fourth, capacity-building funds. Crime laboratories use the availability of Coverdell funding to aid in funding the non-DNA disciplines in training, backlog reduction, and the purchase of equipment. While Coverdell has been authorized at $35 million, in the last few years crime laboratories have received less than half of this money. And, indeed, in the 2014 budget, Coverdell has zero allocation. We are frustrated by the lack of attention to our significant backlogs in non-DNA disciplines, such as drugs, toxicology, and latent prints.

Fifth, while we support the role of NIST in advancing standards and the role of the NSF in research, we remain convinced that the Department of Justice must remain involved in this process and provide the leadership to ensure that the science, standards, training, and education are not only applicable to the mission of providing scientific analysis to the criminal justice system but able to ensure that the grants meet the needs of the community.

We believe the argument that forensics should be removed from law enforcement gets confused with how the crime laboratories should be led. We also believe that forensics should not be removed from law enforcement in its entirety. The accreditation process protects the administrative independence of laboratories.

Mr. Chairman, while we are optimistic about the creation of the National Commission on Forensic Science, we must admit that we have concerns after seeing the charter signed by the Attorney General.

First, the Commission is bound by FACA rules. This would mean state and locals do not have a voice in regards to any outcomes from the Commission.

Second, it will not be developing or recommending guidance regarding digital evidence. Is digital evidence not as important a forensic discipline as DNA analysis? Digital evidence includes the analysis of cell phones and computers. Most of these cases involve homicides, sexual assaults, and white-collar crime.

Should digital evidence not be accredited, adhere to quality assurance systems, or receive training, and is research not important? Currently, digital evidence is seen as forensic in nature and includes its own Scientific Working Group on Digital Evidence. If it is not considered a forensic discipline, we will be sitting here 10 years from now discussing why it was not considered a forensic discipline.

Last, voluntary accreditation for crime labs over the last several years has increased dramatically. Within the next 3 years, all crime laboratories will fall under ISO 17025, which include 400 international standards.

CFSO supports mandated accreditation for crime laboratories in order to ensure standards are adhered to and a quality product exists, but we are very opposed to starting over. Crime laboratories ultimately serve the criminal justice system and the public at large.

Thank you for allowing me to testify today. And, Mr. Chairman, I will be submitting more detailed reporting for the record.

[The prepared statement of Ms. Spriggs follows:]

PREPARED STATEMENT OF JILL SPRIGGS, SECRETARY, CONSORTIUM OF FORENSIC SCIENCE ORGANIZATIONS

Mr. Chairman, Ranking Member and Members of the Committee:

Thank you for asking me to testify before this Committee on matters of forensic science. My name is Jill Spriggs and I am the Crime Laboratory Director for the Office of the District Attorney, Sacramento County, Laboratory of Forensic Services. I am also the Past President of the American Society of Crime Laboratory Directors. In my career, I have overseen the daily operations of both a state and local crime laboratory. Therefore, I come from a unique perspective where I can address forensic issues from both a state and local position. Today, I am here representing the Consortium of Forensic Science Organizations or CFSO which represents over 12,000 forensic science providers.

As you know, the National Academies released in February 2009, a critique or report on the state of forensic science in this Nation. This report distills down into two operational and scientific needs:

1. Need for standardization in education, training and forensic science delivery
2. Need for resources across the forensic science community.

In fact, the forensic science provider community requested Federal legislation to provide guidance and leadership to our community in response to this report and still four years later this has not happened. In the absence of legislation, the Executive Branch has taken numerous efforts to reshape forensic science such as the creation of the National Commission on Forensic Science. I would like to take this opportunity to lay out for this Committee what we believe to be the greatest challenges facing the forensic community and solutions to solve them.

First, while we do believe the Federal Government should be involved in state and local forensic science to maintain consistency and guidance, we do not believe a Federal oversight organization should be created. Any solution needs to understand the important role of state and local labs. While the work the crime laboratory performs is ultimately the same, differences among the state jurisdictions need to be considered and there is not a one size fits all approach that will work. We believe and strongly support the creation of an Office of Forensic Science in the Department of Justice to coordinate and lead on such matters of accreditation, training, education, certification and resource allocation.

Second, many seem to believe there currently exist no standards or training or education in forensic science. This could not be further from the truth. There are currently 22 Scientific Working Groups or SWGs who build consensus standards in the specific forensic disciplines they represent, as well as training guidelines and improvement in practices in the disciplines themselves. Federal, state and local forensic scientists and other experts are represented on the SWGs, as well as academia, attorneys, judges, private laboratory scientists and independent consultants. Historically, these SWGs have operated on very slim budgets and have succeeded in bringing to the forensic disciplines the much needed structure. Why is the administration budgeting a program to create working groups that many believe will undo the work of the SWGs? An inordinate amount of money to start over is being proposed in the 2014 Federal budget. CFSO supports NIST advising the SWG groups in order to give the SWGs the much needed support but to start over and reinvent the wheel is not needed and costly. This will prove extremely disruptive to the scientific community as it waits years for new standards to be disseminated and vetted.

Third, research is an absolutely critical part of how we advance our science as forensic science is just that—a science. Research is critical but it has to be in the context of all the requirements of the forensic science community. What is needed in the forensic community is applied science and by that I mean science that is taken from basic research so that it can be applied in a crime laboratory.

Fourth, capacity building funds. Crime laboratories use the availability of Coverdell funding to aid in funding the non-DNA disciplines in training, backlog reduction and the purchase of equipment. While Coverdell has been authorized at $35 million, in the last few years crime laboratories have received less than half of this money. And indeed in the 2014 budget, Coverdell has a zero allocation. We applaud the efforts to provide us more resources but we are frustrated by the lack of attention to our significant backlogs in non-DNA disciplines such as drugs, toxicology and latent prints.

Fifth, while we support the role of NIST in advancing standards and the role of the NSF in research, we remain convinced that the Department of Justice must remain involved in this process and provide the leadership to ensure that the science, standards, training and education are not only applicable to the mission of providing scientific analysis to the criminal justice system but also to ensure that the grants meet the needs of the community. We believe the argument that forensics should be removed from law enforcement gets confused with how the crime laboratory should be led. We also believe that forensics should not be removed from law enforcement in its entirety. The accreditation process protects the administrative independence of laboratories.

Mr. Chairman, while we are optimistic about the creation of a National Commission on Forensic Science we must admit that we have concerns after seeing the Charter signed by the Attorney General. First, the Commission is bound by FACA rules. This would mean State and Locals do not have a voice in regards to any outcomes from the Commission. Second, it will not be developing or recommending guidance regarding digital evidence. Is digital evidence not as important a forensic discipline as DNA analysis? Digital evidence includes the analysis of cell phones and computers. Most of these cases involve homicides, sexual assaults and white collar crime. Should digital evidence not be accredited, adhere to a quality assurance system or receive training and is research not important? Currently, digital evidence is seen as "forensic" in nature and includes its own Scientific Working Group on Digital Evidence (SWGDE). If it is not considered a forensic discipline, we will be sitting here ten years from now discussing why it was not considered a forensic discipline.

Further, in the past year, several news articles have been written regarding the state of forensic science, including many this week. As we have stated earlier forensic science, like any science, evolves and advances. With the more widespread use of DNA analysis over the last 15–20 years, the incidence of exonerations should decline over time. The advances in DNA are phenomenal as opposed to the old ABO Typing in which 45 percent of the population had Type O blood.

Lastly, voluntary accreditation for crime labs over the last several years has increased dramatically. Within the next three years, all laboratories will fall under ISO 17025 which include over 400 international standards. With ISO 17025 accreditation, cradle to grave documentation exists in crime laboratories where it did not before. CFSO supports mandated accreditation for crime laboratories in order to ensure standards are adhered to and a quality product exists but we are very opposed to starting all over. We should begin with what we have and advance it with the science.

Crime laboratories ultimately serve the criminal justice system and the public at large. The public deserves the best a crime laboratory has to offer and assurance the work coming out of crime laboratories is of the highest quality. Thank you for allowing me to testify today.

The CHAIRMAN. Thank you very much.

Maybe I should just take from what Ms. Spriggs said and maybe get to the heart of the matter.

There seems to be a general rejection by you of a national commission, a sense that you can't apply one standard to all situations and it is not a cookie-cutter business. That is the same argument they used in the health-care bill, and of course they are probably correct in that.

But I had thought in my interest in forensics that—and our state university is working really, really hard on this—that there are some things which have to be deemed to be true or untrue, accurate or inaccurate, scientific or unscientific, no matter whether they are done in Charleston, West Virginia, or in Tuscaloosa, Alabama—in other words, that science is science.

You would argue, perhaps, that a hair follicle is subject to local scientific analysis from the law enforcement folks and that there is not much that a national forensics commission—I just want to get into this subject, because there seems to be tension between the two. Not between the first three witnesses, but between you, ma'am, and the idea that the truth in forensics varies, can vary and should vary, according to where it is done, which was not my understanding of what at least I had to say and my understanding of what others had to say.

Could any of you sort of discuss that?

Mr. BROMWICH. Well, let me start.

I agree with you; there is only one set of scientific standards, validated by basic and applied research. And we shouldn't have a Federal system where you have different standards that are applied because of where a crime arises. I am not sure that is what Dr. Spriggs was saying, but if it was, I disagree with that.

I do think that there is a crying need for Federal leadership and funding on these issues, particularly in the area of basic research, applied research, standards-setting, and so forth. And I do disagree with Dr. Spriggs that basic research needn't play a huge role in this. She stressed applied research. You need both.

I think some of the disciplines that we all took for granted and that we viewed as telling the truth, like fingerprint analysis, have been under attack recently because they have been found not to be as foolproof as we thought. There was the highly publicized case about a decade ago involving Mr. Mayfield from Oregon, where the FBI misidentified Mr. Mayfield as the source of a print in a terrorism case.

So I think there is an absolutely pressing need for both applied research but also basic research and standards-setting on a national level.

The CHAIRMAN. Does one have to choose one mode or the other? Are they meldable, or are they not?

Mr. BROMWICH. Talking about basic research and applied research?

The CHAIRMAN. Yes.

Mr. BROMWICH. You need both. You absolutely need both.

The CHAIRMAN. Anybody else care to—you know what I am——

Ms. SPRIGGS. I——

The CHAIRMAN.—getting at. I have so many examples, as I am sure that the other Senators here do too, of where you have constituencies or organizations which traditionally —I mean, for example, I remember in West Virginia when I was Governor, one of the hardest things was to get counties to agree on basic practices of what sheriffs did. It was just really hard. Everybody had their own way of doing things, and they stuck with those things.

And, I mean, we built an academy for training sheriffs and put up all 55 of their county badges and all kinds of things to try to create goodwill and cooperation. And now there is a lot less of that competition and an understanding that there are sort of common standards that need to be adhered to.

I don't want to over-stress my point, and I am certainly using up my time. But I just felt in you, Ms. Spriggs, a sense that, well, our budget got cut here and our budget got cut there. And everybody is getting cut everywhere—everybody. And that you don't want to have a national commission.

What is dangerous about a national commission to you?

Ms. SPRIGGS. First, let me start with the standards. I am sorry if I have been confusing.

If analysis is performed—let's take, for example, drug analysis. Whether it is performed in Sacramento County on a white powder such as cocaine versus the analysis performed in Florida, the basic analysis is still the same.

What the one-size-does-not-fit-all goes to is the state jurisdictions and what they would see as a reasonable quantity of cocaine. So that is what I mean by a one-size-does-not-fit-all.

The CHAIRMAN. Yes, I don't know how that fits into forensics.

But, in any event, my time is gone, and Senator Thune.

Senator THUNE. Thank you, Mr. Chairman.

And I want to just kind of follow up on that. But, Ms. Spriggs, in your testimony you expressed concerns about the charter for the new national commission. And, again, I would just ask you if you could elaborate a little bit on those concerns, specifically with regard to the participation opportunities for state and local practitioners.

Ms. SPRIGGS. We do applaud the Executive Branch for taking a leadership role in the National Commission on Forensic Science, although we feel that it would be best to have an office of forensic science under the Department of Justice, since that is a judicial system where we apply forensics.

But with the issue of the National Commission, where we see two key, important things that concern us are: one, the imposed FACA rules.

This means that state and locals will not have a way of vetting what comes out of that Commission. So when you talk about research and you talk about presenting research and you present it to different conferences, what you are doing is you are getting feedback from other parties so that you can have questions regarding the research. This is not going to happen on anything that comes out of those commissions because of the FACA rules imposed on that for state and local communities. We want to see what comes out of that Commission and vet it before it is imposed.

Second, we feel strongly regarding digital evidence. Digital evidence, under that charter, will not be looked at as a forensic discipline.

If you look at the crime laboratories across the country, digital evidence is one of the places where we have a backlog of cases. It is one of the booming things that we see in our forensic caseload.

I believe the Netherlands paper also talked about that. So not to include that as far as research, training, standards-setting, to us, brings harm to the discipline of digital evidence.

Senator THUNE. To your knowledge, how much does it cost to operate the scientific working groups at DOJ?

Ms. SPRIGGS. Approximately $150,000 was the cost to operate the Scientific Working Group on the DNA Analysis Methods.

Senator THUNE. And how does that compare to the funding the administration has proposed for NIST to do its own standards-related work?

Ms. SPRIGGS. As opposed to funding for NIST, NIST has been allocated at $3 million, looking at the new budget, if that were to go through.

Senator THUNE. Are those duplicative efforts? I mean, do they actually serve different or do they serve complementary purposes?

Ms. SPRIGGS. They serve differently in that NIST will be starting scientific guidance groups, which will actually reinvent and take over those SWGs and redo the standards. And we feel that while NIST should play a part in SWGs, it should not take those standards and redo them.

Senator THUNE. The National Academies report recommended, and I quote, that "forensic science laboratories should be independent of or autonomous within law enforcement agencies." end quote.

How do you foster that sort of administrative independence at your lab?

Ms. SPRIGGS. We foster that by ISO accreditation, accreditation to the ISO 17025 standards. Within those standards are—and Standard 4.0.

When an assessment or an audit is done, the laboratory will be looked at in regards to those particular standards. One is, does everybody understand their role, the parent organization as well as the crime laboratory? Two, is it an autonomous relationship? Three, is there undue influence? And four is policies and procedures, do they identify bias?

We also do this by, every case that goes out the door is technically reviewed and administratively really reviewed. Do the results in the case notes support the conclusions?

Also, remember, the notes are also discoverable, as well as we encourage prosecutors and defense attorneys to sit down with the crime labs and go through the case before they even go to court.

Also, one of the other ways that we do it is through, again, discovery.

So these are just some of the things that we look at so that there isn't undue influence and bias. We also train our crime labs in bias. We train them in ethics. That is part of our accreditation also.

Senator THUNE. Mr. Tsin-A-Tsoi, the fragmentation that you refer to in your testimony seems to be inherent and fundamental to our country's system of state and local jurisdictions. How does the criminal justice system and forensic science infrastructure in the Netherlands differ from that here in the United States?

Mr. TSIN-A-TSOI. Well, it is a small country, Senator.

[Laughter.]

Mr. TSIN-A-TSOI. That helps.

But also we do have other organizations within the Netherlands that do forensic investigations. The NFI, though, is the prime service provider, so to speak, for law enforcement agencies. We are, however, independent of them. And we also do cases for other countries, and we also do cases for other government agencies than just the law enforcement agencies.

Senator THUNE. Can you describe what you have done with NIST on behalf of the NFI?

Mr. TSIN-A-TSOI. Well, actually, that is just starting up right now. And, actually, later this week or next week, we will have discussions with them.

Senator THUNE. OK.

Mr. TSIN-A-TSOI. Yes.

Senator THUNE. But there is a Memorandum of Understanding on that effort?

Mr. TSIN-A-TSOI. Yes.

Senator THUNE. So that hasn't really gotten under way yet or commenced.

Mr. TSIN-A-TSOI. Well, we have to define what exactly we are going to do about standards-setting. From our point of view, as a forensic community, we have a standards problem. And we want to solve that and want to work on that very hard. And we know that NIST is an absolutely top-notch organization, the state-of-the-art worldwide, and this is why we tried to get in contact with them. And they were interested, as well.

Senator THUNE. OK. Thank you.

Mr. Chairman, my time has expired. Thank you.

The CHAIRMAN. Thank you, Senator Thune.

Senator Chiesa?

STATEMENT OF HON. JEFF CHIESA, U.S. SENATOR FROM NEW JERSEY

Senator CHIESA. Thank you, Mr. Chairman.

And thank all of you for your testimony.

I know in my own experience of the great pains that the law enforcement community takes to make sure that they get it right. The law enforcement community is there to keep us safe. And I know that anytime you bring a charge against anybody, you really need to have all of your evidence in order and you have to have drawn a conclusion that the case should be brought, because whether or not the case is proven, you have altered that person's life for good.

And I know there is no suggestion here that there is not excellent work being done, but that work, in my experience, has been of the highest quality. I have been extremely proud, whether it was with the FBI or with the state police in New Jersey, extremely proud to work with those law enforcement communities.

But I know that we can always try to strive for a better result and a more complete result and one that reminds the public and ensures the public's trust in the kinds of results that we are getting.

I think Senator Thune made an excellent point earlier, too. And that is, to some extent, scientific evidence, when you call it scientific, can overwhelm the case from the start. Because if a scientist gets up and takes the witness stand, there is a status that that witness has that is different than a lay witness who says, I saw somebody do something.

And I think there is an expectation now, because of the way the cases are portrayed on TV, that if you have three witnesses that saw a crime committed, where is your fingerprint expert, where is your DNA expert? As you know, those are costly things that you can't do in every case. So I understand the balance and the things that have to go into these issues as we develop them.

So let's start with Mr. Bromwich. You talked about investigations that you were involved in. I know you spent part of your life in the world of a prosecutor. What is your sense of the strides that have been made since the investigation in Houston in 1994 to the present? Are we making the kinds of strides you think that are making a difference?

And is the level of commitment here what it should be so that when we bring scientific evidence into a case, with the kind of weight that it carries, that it is being brought in an appropriate and a complete way?

Mr. BROMWICH. Senator, has progress been made in the last 20 years? Undoubtedly, I think in part through the awareness of the way things can go wrong if they are not done right.

But are we where we need to be? No. All you have to do is pick up the newspaper to see about crime lab problems that have arisen just recently in Texas, in Minnesota, in Massachusetts, in New York. They just happen too frequently.

And as you know because you were a prosecutor, if an examiner has been found to do bad work in one case or engaged in intentional misconduct in one case, that imperils scores of cases. They are going through that right now in Massachusetts, where they had a drug examiner, and they are having to reexamine literally thousands of cases.

When I was a prosecutor a long time ago, even before you were, putting in scientific evidence was viewed as routine, almost automatic. We viewed the expert witnesses as our coaches and tutors, and they told us what to ask them and they gave us what their answers would be.

We are removed from that but not far enough removed from that. And by that I mean there is a tremendous amount of additional education that needs to go on to train prosecutors, to train defense counsel, to train judges in some of the basics of forensics.

In our Houston investigation, 2005 to 2007, we found that defense counsel almost never challenged forensic experts, even when there was a lot of information in the public sector suggesting that they were doing——

Senator CHIESA. That is a little bit of a separate issue, though, right? I mean, that is on the obligation of the defense counsel. And I appreciate everything you are saying. I am going to run out of time in a minute.

When we view these cases retrospectively and you talk about the things that you are talking about, someone acting for the wrong, fraudulent motive, whatever it is, someone acting incompetently, I think those are different things, right? Someone is motivated by, I want to—there is a horrific crime that occurs; there is enormous pressure on the prosecutor to stay the fears in that community.

When you talk about these national standards, are they getting at the training that these folks are going to get?

Because I know—and maybe Ms. Spriggs can talk to this, as well—what you worry about when you are bringing cases is, is my evidence going to get to me when I get to trial, whether it is a speedy trial issue so your case has to be brought in a certain amount of time.

So are there any concerns that these national standards are going to create delays that the defense counsel may use then to put further pressure on prosecutors that they are not bringing their cases fast enough?

Mr. BROMWICH. I don't have that concern, Senator. I think the work is going to continue to be done at the local level, and the speed will be the same.

Senator CHIESA. Thank you, Mr. Chairman. My time is up.

The CHAIRMAN. You are welcome. And you are new, so you get a couple of minutes extra.

[Laughter.]

Senator CHIESA. Well, thank you.

Ms. Spriggs, one of the things I have thought about when you are saying one size doesn't fit all, if you have a state like New Jersey, we can centralize a crime lab in one location and multiple areas of the state can have access to that location. If I was in a state like Montana, where it is geographically enormous, they may not have the ability to have one location to do all of those things.

Is there any concern on your part, in terms of your one size doesn't fit all, that if we create these national standards we are going to have problems standing up enough locations to serve different size communities with different kinds of needs?

Ms. SPRIGGS. I think with the national standards what we are talking about is having an underlying national standard. So, like, right now we have what is called the DNA Advisory Board standards that every laboratory that is doing DNA in this country must follow. So those are the standards that we are talking about, not so much the legal standards as to what is a usable quantity or things like that.

I can tell you, I oversaw 13 laboratories in California and I oversaw over 40 counties within California. Each county had their own jurisdiction with a little bit of how they wanted to report out results as far as drugs go. Some people thought this amount was a usable quantity, and some didn't. But the underlying science of how we got to what that drug was was the same.

Now, you asked Mr. Bromwich about, is the defense using these standards to swap out speedy trials and because of the standards it is taking longer. That is true in some cases. With the ISO accreditation, we do have cradle-to-grave documentation now. And a lot of the cases that Mr. Bromwich talked about in Massachusetts and Minnesota, they are not accredited. They are not accredited to these international standards, ISO 17025.

Another issue that really needs to be brought up, and it is one that Dr. Tsoi brought up, is management of a crime laboratory. While you see a lot of these issues, a lot of these issues are not so much quality issues, like in Massachusetts and Minnesota; it is a management issue. It is lack of management—management looking at backlogs, management in looking at what are the differences between people who are out putting cases.

So if I have someone in a drug section who is putting out 50 cases a month but I have someone else putting out 300 cases a month, that to me is going to query something in my head that, okay, there is something going on.

So there is another issue here that needs to be brought up, and that is a lack of management of crime laboratories. And for that, remember, we are taking a lot of bench scientists and putting them in as managers who sometimes don't have the qualifications to be a manager or to look at backlogs, look at statistics, how much is a case costing per case, things like that.

Senator CHIESA. Thank you.

Thank you, Mr. Chairman.

The CHAIRMAN. Thank you very much.

Senator Warner?

STATEMENT OF HON. MARK WARNER, U.S. SENATOR FROM VIRGINIA

Senator WARNER. Thank you, Mr. Chairman. Appreciate you holding this hearing. I don't know a lot about this subject. I know you have had a great deal of interest.

But I am actually asking for an update, because when I was Governor, I had two remarkable circumstances. One that I think has actually become somewhat known in the science, the one with Mary Jane Burton, a woman in our lab who had literally attached DNA swabs to thousands of cases that she had worked on before DNA evidence had moved ahead. And suddenly we discovered this, and, you know, what do you do with it?

We went out and finally went back and checked all those cases, exonerated a number of people. We found, actually, that there were then—and I would be curious for your commentary on this—people had been exonerated, but there was no procedure in place to make sure that information, if it got to the prosecution, actually got relayed then back to the person who potentially was exonerated.

We had a similar case that was even higher-profile where, actually, somebody had been executed. The cover of Time magazine said, this man is innocent. People had spent years trying to prove his innocence.

And as a supporter of the death penalty, and any Governor who has gone through that most ultimate decision, there was DNA evidence that retained, there was question about chain of custody, and the question of, do you go back and retest years later after the execution and reopen that? I thought, as someone who had made that ultimate decision, not on this individual, but you had to retest. It ended up proving the guilt of the individual.

But I just wonder whether these procedures—this was 7, 8, 9 years ago on these cases—you still read about this stuff, Senator, as you mentioned. But have the procedures moved forward where there are kind of accepted codes of conduct?

And I heard from my staff that there was some question about national versus local standards. I would hope that would be about procedural standards, not about national versus local science. The science ought to be science, and we should not be afraid of where that evidence leads us.

So I hope somebody can clear up my staff's comments to me, one, about the distinction, that if there is a debate between a national standard versus a local standard, that that is about procedures. I actually believe that this should be looked at on a national basis and science ought to trump all. But there is not a question about the underlying science in terms of different standards, are there?

And then, second, have some of these, you know—— because these incidents are kind of a little bit worn off, I think you would need to have some level of national procedures because you would want to have that guidance if it becomes a case of first instance.

A bit of a rambling question, I know.

Mr. BROMWICH. Let me answer the second part of your question first. And you are really alluding to situations where problems are discovered, either with the work of a particular analyst or a particular type of analysis, what kind of system is in place to inform the relevant people, namely defendants and defense counsel, that they might have an issue that they need to do something about.

I think it is getting better in some respects, but there are still noteworthy instances where things don't work the way they should. So, for example, I mentioned at the outset the investigation my agency did of the FBI Lab back in the period of 1995 to 1997. The Justice Department set up a task force within the department whose task was to review cases worked by the examiners whose competence and conduct we are reviewed during our investigation.

In a series of articles in *The Washington Post* within the last 6 months or so, it was disclosed that, in fact, that work didn't get pushed forward, that defense counsel were not notified in a systematic way. And, in fact, that process is now the subject of a follow up inspector general review.

I like to think that is not typical, but it happens. And I think one of the things that every jurisdiction, national, state, and local, needs to do is when examples of this come to light, there has to be a sustained, coherent process to make sure that the relevant people are notified. That doesn't happen enough.

Senator WARNER. Are you saying there is not even kind of the protocol standards, even if they are not legally enforceable, that are kind of viewed as traditional or accepted rules of the road, in effect, in terms of process or protocol?

Mr. BROMWICH. There are post-conviction processes in all 50 states, and they differ. But I think the kind of situation you faced when you were Governor of Virginia, how do you deal with a particular examiner who did something they shouldn't have done, how do you followup, what kinds of testing do you do, what kind of notification process, that is not at all standardized.

And I think in each instance when it comes up it is treated as a one-off by whatever jurisdiction is dealing with it. It is unfortunate, but I think it is true.

Ms. SPRIGGS. May I add a comment?

Senator WARNER. Please.

Ms. SPRIGGS. As far as the case where the swabs were in the case file, I don't think that would happen today. We have policies and procedures in place that are part of our accreditation that talks about what we are to do with evidence, make sure there is a chain of custody, all of that. As well as, when an assessor or an auditor comes through, they actually take case files and take a sampling to make sure that you are following your policies.

The underlying science that you were talking about is the same throughout the crime laboratory systems throughout the nation. The underlying science is the same. So if I have been confusing in that message, I am sorry.

Senator WARNER. But I guess what I would just say, Ms. Spriggs, is that, you know, in the case of Mary Jane Burton it was swabs that were discovered in 2003–2004. I, again, caught a bit of your testimony just as I walked in. You know, that was then. Today it may not be swabs; today it may be digital. Or there may be a host of residual information that we are not fully aware of as the science moves forward.

It would seem to me, even if it was not legally enforceable, the notion that there ought to be some level of protocols so that policymakers, prosecutors, others, you know, don't all kind of see these as cases of first impression. Even if you don't have to follow the rules, it just seems to me would make some sense, and it would make some sense if you had some national effort to try to at least inform those policymakers.

So I sure as heck would love to have had in both cases, both in the reexamining of the already-executed individual and the case of Mary Jane Burton, someplace to look. I think I got to the right decision point, but I would have liked to have had some guidance. I could have gotten through a lot less sleepless nights, particularly on the reopening of the case of the executed individual.

Ms. SPRIGGS. One other item that was brought up, I think by Mr. Bromwich, was, when there is an issue in a crime laboratory, you do have an obligation to notify not only the prosecutor but you do have an obligation to notify the defense.

So when there is an issue in a crime laboratory—let's say there is a mix-up of samples. Because of our ISO accreditation, we do what is called a CAR, a corrective action request, where we follow through. We go back and we look at prior cases; we notify the prosecutor on those cases. Part of that corrective action is notification to the defense community that you have this issue in your laboratory.

And all of that is looked at when an auditor comes in or assessor comes in to do your accreditation.

Senator WARNER. Thank you.

Thank you, Mr. Chairman.

The CHAIRMAN. Thank you, Senator Warner.

There is not much that Senator Warner doesn't know a lot about. [Laughter.]

The CHAIRMAN. I say that sincerely and with respect, as I hope you know.

I am going to do something I have never done before. It is like we are stuck on a record here; it keeps playing the same music.

And to be honest with you, Ms. Spriggs, I have the feeling that you—see, on the one hand, you just in the last answer to Senator

Warner, you said science has to be science all over the country. And when I heard that, I had a good feeling.

More or less everything else you have said, it sounds to me like you are trying to protect a group which you represent as a lobbyist, so to speak, from having to change. Because people genuinely don't like change. That is true in the human race.

And you are talking about budget cuts and process and management and backlogs, all of which are very important. But, to me, the basic question of this hearing, is that science has to be agreed on and that has to be acceptable in every county in every state all over the country, not because there is a law that says there has to be, but it doesn't make any sense for it not to be that way. As Senator Warner said, science is science.

And I think what the question is—I mean, this fellow, Harry Edwards—you claim that the FBI, Ms. Spriggs, that the FBI's SWGs, as you said—actually, it is more helpful to us if you say "scientific working groups"——effectively develop standards and guidelines for the forensic science disciplines, and there are experts who disagree with you.

Judge Harry Edwards, who was one of the leading authors of the report which I held up, has stated that SWGs are of questionable value. He says that, among other problems, SWGs do not meet regularly, their standards are too vague, and they don't try to determine if anybody is actually implementing their recommendations. Now, I have no idea whether that is true or not, but he is a leading Federal judge and he is a leading expert on forensic evidence.

So I am a little bit in a state of confusion. Because when you say science has to be science everywhere, my head would nod. And, to me, that is what this hearing is about. But I may be missing something.

You, sir, are not saying much.

[Laughter.]

The CHAIRMAN. So what I would like to have during my time, and I may add on it a couple minutes—that is really the reason I gave him 2 extra minutes.

[Laughter.]

The CHAIRMAN. Kind of duke it out amongst you. What is the problem here? What is the basic disagreement?

Dr. SCHMUNK. Senator, since you did look at me, I will respond from the medical examiner community.

Our issue is not so much that—I think many of the crime labs have wonderful accreditation standards. Our problem throughout the country is there are no standards and there are no accreditations for the vast majority of offices in this country.

So keep in mind that the medical examiner, in at least a death case, is going to be the one that collects the specimens that we send to the crime lab. If there is no coherent policy to collect DNA, if there is no coherent policy to collect fingernail scrapings, for example, then the crime labs will have nothing to work with.

So my problem with the medical examiner situation is that we have most of the offices in the country that are working under policies that have been developed in their own offices, but there are no accreditation standards that they follow.

The CHAIRMAN. And you are not saying that just from an academic point of view. You are saying it from an accuracy-times-accuracy point of view.

Dr. SCHMUNK. Correct.

The CHAIRMAN. Yes.

Our Netherlands expert?

I am just trying to find out what I thought this was going to be about as a hearing and what it turns out it may be about as a hearing. I need to get that settled. I have all these questions I want to ask, but I can't get past this. Maybe it is my limitation.

Please, sir.

Mr. TSIN-A-TSOI. I am not a forensic scientist by background, by training. I do have a physics Ph.D., but I joined this sector just 6 years ago when I became CEO.

What I noticed was that, really, it is a rather closed field, a rather protective-of-itself field. And I think that is probably one of the reasons that these discussions lead to some resistance within the field. And I had this resistance within our own organization as well, in the beginning especially.

Also, yes, some forensic disciplines are really fundamentally subjective right at the moment. They depend very much on the judgment of individual professionals. And, in the past and maybe still, that is something that is tacitly welcomed by some of these professionals, because, you know, it places a very large premium on their personal opinion on the case.

And saying that their work is not scientific—because that is, then, what you are saying, isn't it? What we are saying here, almost all of us, is that, well, you know, maybe some of the work you have done in the past presenting yourself as a scientist is maybe not so scientific after all. And that is a big thing to say. That might also play a role in this. And, actually, let me put it like this. In the Netherlands, in my institute, yes, this has played a big role, in the beginning especially.

And also, a final point: The way forensic science came about was not really as a science maybe from the beginning. It started out as something extra on top of normal, traditional investigative methods, and it grew out from that kind of position. This is the reason probably why many forensic institutes or forensic laboratories are still part of the police.

I certainly agree with the statement in the National Academy of Sciences' report that it is better to have forensic institutes to be independent of the customers that they serve. And from the Government's point of view—I don't believe that people are biased, but, you know, if you are a part of a specific organization and you work always only for that organization which has specific tasks in society, that tends to have a certain influence. It doesn't have to be obvious but it can be very tacit.

So what I am trying to say here is that forensic science has not evolved in science, it has evolved in police. And that has had a very dramatic influence on what we call forensic science.

Thank you.

The CHAIRMAN. So, in a sense, you would say that—oh, Senator Blumenthal has come in. And he knows everything about everything.

[Laughter.]

The CHAIRMAN. You do. I am glad you came.

I am struggling here as best as I can. I am neither a lawyer nor a scientist, and I didn't get very good algebra marks. But I care about this subject immensely.

And, in a sense, then, you are saying that there is a science, there is an answer. And in a DNA case, maybe that is true, but in some other—you are not saying that?

OK. Well, whatever.

[Laughter.]

The CHAIRMAN. But that it has evolved on a local basis, therefore in variation.

And as you watch—granted, these are some of the episodes on television, but as you watch some of these programs, all kinds of things enter in. I mean, there are political pressures. Is somebody going to pursue this or pursue that? Would that mean they would lose their standing? What about a judge?

You know, I mean, there are a lot of moving parts in a highly tense world of, if you go to prison, you don't go to prison, what it is that is used as evidence has to be absolutely right. And to the extent that science is involved in that evidence, it has to be absolutely right.

Have I said nothing, or have I said something?

Mr. BROMWICH. I think you have said something.

[Laughter.]

Mr. BROMWICH. I agree with almost everything that Mr. Tsoi said. And I am not a forensic scientist, and I am not even a scientist. But I have learned a lot about the way forensic science is applied in our forensic labs through the investigations I talked about at the outset. And I learned it from forensic scientists who were part of our investigative teams and who provided me with a lot of insight into the way forensic science is currently practiced and the way it should be practiced.

I think there is resistance in the existing forensic science community because, up until very recently, it was a bit of a closed guild and it was not subjected to a lot of external scrutiny. That has changed very substantially with the development of DNA and the exposure through DNA analysis of some of the flaws and mistakes that the other forensic sciences and analysts in those forensic sciences have committed.

So I very much agree with Mr. Tsoi that there is an insularity to the forensic science community. But that is not to devalue the hard and good work that many of the people in the community do. And it is not to suggest, as I think Ms. Spriggs was doing, that anybody is suggesting that you burn the current system to the ground.

You are really talking about a house, if you will, whose foundations are sagging and there are problems with it, and you want to bolster it, you want to support it, you want to build firmer foundations for it based on science. Everyone is the winner if you do that.

Ms. SPRIGGS. I believe we are pretty much on target, all of us. And let me explain what I mean.

When you are building a house and it is falling down and you want to bolster it, what do you do first? You want to check with the person who owns the house and help them develop the plans for the new house in case you want to change a room or you want to do something.

We support the commission. We support national standards. What we want to do is be a part of those. Right now FACA——

The CHAIRMAN. Who says you are not?

Ms. SPRIGGS. Because rules are imposed on the——

The CHAIRMAN. The commission isn't even fully appointed yet.

Ms. SPRIGGS. But it is going to be imposed. If you read the charter, FACA rules are imposed.

We want to be part of the solution. We want to have a place at the table to give our community a chance to vet. State and locals need a chance to help develop these standards.

The CHAIRMAN. I don't disagree with you. And I have no idea what a FACA thing is. I hope it is not a dirty word. But I have no idea what it is, but I——

Mr. BROMWICH. Senator, it is——

The CHAIRMAN.—don't want you to hide behind it.

Mr. BROMWICH. I maybe know too much about FACAs because I set one up recently at the Department of the Interior. I am not aware of any limitation on the involvement of state and local personnel.

The CHAIRMAN. Nor am I.

Ms. SPRIGGS. Well, I can only tell you that when——

The CHAIRMAN. Let me just read from—excuse me—from the Commission charter.

We have gotten way off here, Senator Blumenthal.

He was an attorney general for 29 years, so don't discount him, all right?

[Laughter.]

The CHAIRMAN. This is "Membership and Designation": The Commission will be co-chaired by a senior DOJ official and a senior NIST official." That is both sides. You are with DOJ, and then others might be with NIST, including me.

"The Commission shall recommend whether the Attorney General shall endorse guidance and practice guidelines for DOJ laboratories and forensic-science-related policy initiatives."

And then, to the point: "The Commission will consist of approximately 30 members appointed by the Attorney General in consultation"—in consultation—"with the Director of NIST"—OK?—"and co-chairs of the Commission. The Commission members will be selected to achieve a balance of backgrounds, experience, viewpoints, expertise, and scientific, legal, law enforcement, academic, and advocacy professions."

It is hard to argue that the state and local reps won't be included in this list. And it is not even done yet.

Ms. SPRIGGS. If you look at number two under "authority"——

The CHAIRMAN. I am going to call on Senator Blumenthal——

Ms. SPRIGGS. Oh, I am sorry.

The CHAIRMAN.—because I am at 9 minutes, which is a criminal act.

[Laughter.]

STATEMENT OF HON. RICHARD BLUMENTHAL, U.S. SENATOR FROM CONNECTICUT

Mr. BLUMENTHAL. Mr. Chairman, I would be happy to yield to you to continue——

The CHAIRMAN. You can go ahead.

Senator BLUMENTHAL.—your questioning. Thank you.

First of all, let me thank you for having this hearing and for your dedication to this cause, which, as you have very, very accurately stated, is really profoundly important to the quality of justice in our country but also in many, many other ways.

We had a hearing just days ago on the derailment and collision of two trains in the Bridgeport area of Connecticut involving the application of forensic science to determine and investigate what was the cause, what should be the consequences in terms of holding either companies or individuals accountable. So forensic science has far-reaching and profound effects in our justice system and in many other areas of our life.

And I want to thank the Chairman for his bill, the Forensic Science and Standards Act of 2012, which I think advanced this debate very substantially and, in fact, I think, led to the creation of the Commission, which was one of the provisions of the bill, and other progress that I think has flowed from his focus on this area.

And thank each of you for your dedication to raising the bar, raising the standard, and assuring that there is more professionalism.

My view, as a former United States attorney, a prosecutor for 4½ years in the Federal courts, and then as Attorney General of our state of Connecticut, is that the science is, in fact, progressing. And the best evidence of it is the new institute at the University of New Haven, which has been headed by Dr. Henry Lee of New Haven. And I was pleased to recommend him for the Commission, as a matter of fact.

The Commission and Dr. Lee have been tireless advocates for making sure that we have proper accreditation and that there are proficiency tests and certifications created and standardized in this area. And he was one of the first to implement laboratory standards so that we avoid some of the pitfalls that the 2009 report of the National Academy of Sciences brought to light.

So my question, first of all for Dr. Schmunk, is, how can we increase the number of trained pathologists devoted to forensic science? Or, really, to the entire panel if you have views on this subject, the number of pathologists.

Do we need more residency slots? What can be done to spur all of the professions involved—it is really multidisciplinary—to not only recognize but incentivize people to specialize in this area?

Dr. SCHMUNK. I will touch on your last point first, and that is incentivization. And one of the incentives that can be given—a medical examiner is basically a public servant, and loan forgiveness for the enormous amount that each of these students have for their medical education would go a long way to convince them to go into medical examiner, forensic pathology, rather than diagnostic radiology, where they could make a lot more money but might not have their student loans forgiven.

We are approaching this, along with the College of American Pathologists and other professional organizations, from the ground up. We are encouraging medical students to have rotations in forensic sciences, all the way up through students that are currently in pathology residency programs. And so there are many things that can be done.

One of the problems with the training programs in forensic pathology, unlike with most graduate medical education, which has been a problem with funding throughout the past several years in general but especially with regard to forensic pathology, many of our training programs do not exist in institutions where there is Federal money pumped in for graduate medical education. We are at the county and state level, and so the money that comes for training has to come from the local taxpayers.

Senator BLUMENTHAL. Do you think that HHS, the Department of Health and Human Services, can and should be supporting more programming that provides those incentives for medical students to choose forensic pathology at a higher rate?

Dr. SCHMUNK. Yes. And one of the things that is in my prepared statement that I think the chair will have a strong interest in, being on Finance, is that there is an issue with payment for death investigations and autopsies. Many years ago, the accreditation council removed the requirement of 20 percent autopsies. So, basically, we are now down to less than 10 percent of deaths in the country are autopsied, and most of those are done by forensic pathologists in medical examiner and coroner systems.

If the autopsy was a compensable expense to these hospitals, which it is not currently—one of the very few things that Medicare will not pay for is an autopsy. Once you are dead, the Federal Government pretty much does not care about you.

If we would put money into Medicare and convince private insurance to pay for autopsies as a quality assurance measure, which we know it is, that would go a long way to funding many of these programs, including the education of our physicians into forensic pathology.

Senator BLUMENTHAL. Very interesting point.

Any other observations on that question?

Mr. BROMWICH. I think it is a broader problem than just pathologists. I think there is a pressing need to provide various kinds of incentives, financial incentives, student loan forgiveness, for the full range of forensic scientists. We need to attract the best and the brightest into these fields, and although things have gotten better, it is not happening enough.

Senator BLUMENTHAL. Well, my time has expired. I will be submitting a number of questions for the record and hope that perhaps you can answer them in writing.

But I really do appreciate your being here. This area is enormously important.

And one of the questions I am going to be submitting is whether there ought to be a Federal agency—and I know that the chairman has asked this question—a Federal agency that oversees the creation of standards and application of forensics. And what drives innovation? A separate question, what drives innovation in this field of forensics? And whether there is a need for public funding in this area.

So thank you very much.

Thank you, Mr. Chairman.

The CHAIRMAN. Thank you, Senator Blumenthal.

Senator Ayotte, can I make one little peep——

Senator AYOTTE. Of course.

The CHAIRMAN.—and then call right on you?

Senator AYOTTE. You can peep.

[Laughter.]

The CHAIRMAN. All right, here is my little peep.

This sort of reminds me of our 4-year, totally unsuccessful to this point, but ultimately it will be, trying to sort out cybersecurity. And cybersecurity has long since displaced al Qaeda as our number one national security threat, et cetera, et cetera, et cetera. It is overwhelming. As the FBI director said, it is the greatest transfer of wealth in the history of the world, as people clean out all of our bank files and information files.

Anyway, one of the things that is agreed on, although the approach to it is not yet agreed on, is that there has to be a private-public partnership in which NIST encourages and is the enabler, not the decider, but enables, encourages people to come together.

Because, as it turns out, a lot of the major companies that are getting clobbered by hacking don't do anything about it because they don't want it known because it might, you know, affect their stock position or whatever. And it is terribly serious. And we go back and forth, and it becomes almost a little bit, you know, ideology. And it shouldn't be.

I do think there is generally agreement that NIST, which as you say, Doctor, is this extraordinarily brilliant and misunderstood Federal agency, that there is a feeling that they should be the ones who convene, enable the public and the private to get together to figure out what are the best ways to put up walls of protection to secure their patents and everything else. And as they put up walls, others will put up higher walls, and then higher and higher you go.

But there has to be a system for that, and somebody has to decide what is a proper standard that somebody needs to meet to say that—and this gets into liability and all kinds of other questions. But it is tricky stuff, but it is desperately important, and we are not grappling with it. And that is frustrating to me, and I am sure it is to my two colleagues here also.

So, I mean, there is a lot of stuff here where you get down to, what is a basic standard, what constitutes a basic standard? How much does one adhere to something called science?

And, with that, I will be quiet and turn to Senator Ayotte.

STATEMENT OF HON. KELLY AYOTTE, U.S. SENATOR FROM NEW HAMPSHIRE

Senator AYOTTE. Thank you, Mr. Chairman.

I want to thank the witnesses for being here.

I was a murder prosecutor. And, Mr. Bromwich, I know you are a former prosecutor. The issue of forensics is very important to the strength of any case, and the validity of forensics is incredibly important to the integrity of the justice system in terms of determining whether a charge will be brought and for providing information to juries so they can decide on the guilt or innocence of individuals.

I certainly, having been a prosecutor, want the juries to focus on the facts of the case. And there is always a lot of time, there can be a lot of time spent, obviously, on cross-examination on issues like certification.

I had a case where it was a very high profile murder case, and I had to defend our lab because they were in certification process but they hadn't completed it. They were going through the ASCLD certification but just hadn't completed it. And they now have completed it, and I am very proud of our laboratory.

So I fully appreciate the importance of certification in the context of even why good laboratories want to voluntarily undertake it.

In the context of thinking about developing national standards, you know, help me understand, do you think that mandatory certification would be more effective? Is there now also an incentive for voluntary certification?

And the one thing that I am hearing, that, you know, we talked to my laboratory director about it, and I am very conscious about this, is that if we impose unfunded mandates on the states on this issue, that we could actually diminish resources that they need in other capacities in the criminal justice system. And I think that is a big challenge.

So I wanted to get your thoughts on those issues, and anyone else who would like to comment. Because this idea of hurting the justice system by imposing requirements that we are not going to back up here, where we are saying it is the national standard and you have to do it, and then they don't have the resources allocated and we don't give them resources.

So resources are always an issue in all of these cases, as you know. They temper what we are able to prosecute. They temper what cases we are able to investigate and the choices that we have to make in cases.

So I will leave that to you, Mr. Bromwich.

Mr. BROMWICH. Senator, it is a big problem, and it is a fair question. I think unfunded mandates in this area are particularly tricky and dangerous given the chronic underfunding of crime labs generally. So I think that is something we need to worry about.

I am in favor of building up the standards through, among other things, the creation of a National Forensic Science Commission that we have been discussing a little bit here today. I do think there is a problem, and we discussed this back and forth before you got here, about the risk of having different standards and, in effect, different science applied in different jurisdictions. I don't think anybody wants that. That is not a desirable thing to have.

And I think it is in everyone's interest to have certification, to have proficiency training, to have accreditation. I think voluntary accreditation has improved things. No one should view a lab that is accredited as one that is going to be guaranteed to be free of problems. That is not what anybody who is part of the lab accreditation process will ever argue.

But I think it is in everyone's interest to continue to build up the scientific basis of the disciplines that forensic scientists use in a laboratory and testify about in court. That is what I understand the chairman has been trying to do through his legislation introduced last session and that he is going to introduce again.

It is harder for forensic scientists than it used to be, but that is not a bad thing. When I was a prosecutor a very long time ago, we received the information the forensic scientists gave us as words from God. And the information that was conveyed in reports and testimony was never challenged, ever, even when it should have been. And I did some investigations, including one in Houston, where the entire criminal defense bar admitted that it just collectively lay down and never challenged unfounded, unscientific testimony that forensic experts were giving.

So there are additional hardships now. The world of practicing criminal defense law is different because people realize that some of these techniques can and should be challenged. But I would argue that is a good thing, not a bad thing.

Senator AYOTTE. I agree with that. I mean, I think that is why we have the Daubert standard, that is why we have vigorous cross-examination.

It is just trying to figure out where—when I served as Attorney General, and then before that being a murder prosecutor, I mean, I was constantly dealing with my lab on the issues of resources as a policymaker, not as a prosecutor but as a policymaker, of how do I get the resources that this lab really needs?

I am a strong fan of my lab. They voluntary undertook ASCLD. They have very high standards. I think that they have integrity, and that is important to the lab. But, that said, it is always a resource challenge. And so what worries me a little bit is that we will do all these things in Washington, and then we will make that challenge even greater. So that is what concerns me.

And so, I know my time is up, but if I could have just one minute?

The CHAIRMAN. Sure.

Senator AYOTTE I just wanted to get your thoughts on this resource challenge and how it does impact the justice system and, really, how do we address it?

Ms. SPRIGGS. I can speak to the resource challenge.

One of the things we do agree on is mandatory accreditation. In the last probably 4 to 5 years, there is a new accreditation. It is called ISO 17025. They are international standards, the same standards that the automobile industry might use. They are not set by the crime laboratories. They are international standards.

A lot of the laboratories have——

Senator AYOTTE. Yes, I am dating myself. I haven't been in the courtroom in a while, so——

Ms. SPRIGGS. That is OK.

A lot of the laboratories have volunteered to get accredited without the additional resources. So in order for a laboratory to be accredited, it is a few hundred thousand dollars per year.

One of the things that helps us in accreditation and helps us is called Coverdell funding, which there is—it is authorized for $35 million. In the last few years, we have not even seen half of that money.

Senator AYOTTE. This funding was very important in my laboratory.

Ms. SPRIGGS. Very important.

Now, I can tell you from a state perspective, I can tell you from a local perspective. I came from a state agency that might get about—I had 450 employees and an $80 million budget that got about $400,000, $500,000 of that Coverdell funding. I am now at a local laboratory, where I only get $20,000 of that funding.

But that $20,000 lets me send people so they can learn about new research, learn about and do training, go to conferences, helps with backlogs, helps with all of that. So even though it is a small amount for my local laboratory now, it really helps out.

So when you look at the funding, we do need funding because we took existing funding so that we can get accredited with the ISO 17025 standards, which are the gold standard, if you want to call them, of accreditation. So, again, that Coverdell funding does help us.

Mr. TSIN-A-TSOI. Can I make a brief remark?

The CHAIRMAN. Please.

Mr. TSIN-A-TSOI. Two brief remarks.

First of all, I would like to say that certification, especially by ISO rules, is not the same as the scientific development that we are talking about. Many labs around the world are ISO-certified, but that has nothing to do with the fact that the science of forensics is not developed as it should be.

The second remark I would like to make is that underfunding, "underfunding," it is just a matter of perspective. The problem is that there is a supply and demand problem here. You have enormous demand, an increasing demand because of technological possibilities of forensic science at laboratories, and the supply, so the funds that are available for these labs, are not commensurate to the demand.

And that is because of the way they are funded, not necessarily because of the size of the funding. What happens usually is that a lab gets a certain amount of money per year, for example, and is then supposed to do all the work that is sent to them for that amount, and that is not possible. Because for the person asking for the investigation of the lab, it is for free. Because the lab is there, so you just send in the DNA, and if you send in twice the total capacity of the lab, that is it. So then the lab is underfunded.

So this is exactly the situation that we had at the NFI in the Netherlands. Our caseload grew in 10 years' time six-fold, but the funding didn't grow six-fold. At a certain point, we had to—well, this is what I meant in my speech, with a more businesslike approach to our customer relations. We made a service-level agreement with our customers which stipulates how much work we can do in what types of areas. And that helped a lot.

And, of course, at the beginning this was difficult for the system as a whole, but in the end everybody is much happier now.

Mr. BROMWICH. This is not really an answer to your question, Senator, but I—I am sorry.

Senator AYOTTE. I just want to make sure it is OK——

The CHAIRMAN. Oh, of course it is.

Senator AYOTTE. OK.

Mr. BROMWICH. I think it is both an amount of resources and also a predictability of resources.

As you probably know from working with your lab, top lab managers spend way too much time trying to get grants to keep their labs going. And that time is taken away from actually managing their people in the lab.

So I don't have an instant solution to the problem, but I just want to identify the problem, that it is both a volume of resources and it is a sustainability and predictability of resources so that the lab knows what it is going to have to allocate.

Senator AYOTTE. Thank you all. You are right.

And thank you, Mr. Chairman.

I think that is the challenge. They spend a lot of time trying to figure out where the next funding source, Federal or otherwise, is going to come from.

Thank you.

The CHAIRMAN. Senator Blumenthal?

Senator BLUMENTHAL. I thank Senator Ayotte for her questions, also as a former prosecutor.

Are there particular areas of forensic science that most trouble you, in terms of the reliability of testimony—fingerprinting, obviously bullet analysis has proven problematic.

If you could identify one, two, three areas that most trouble you in their use in the courtroom, what would they be?

Mr. BROMWICH. For me, hair.

Senator BLUMENTHAL. Hair.

Mr. BROMWICH. Paints and polymers. Other kinds of trace evidence.

Dr. SCHMUNK. For the medical examiner community, I think it is clear that it is child abuse prosecutions, head injury and the science behind that diagnosis.

Senator BLUMENTHAL. Bruises and other physical evidence of head injury or other child abuse.

Dr. SCHMUNK. And the hemorrhages in the eyes, the hemorrhages on the brain, and the tearing of the axons, which can be problematic, especially if the child survives in the hospital for some time.

Ms. SPRIGGS. For me, it would be forensic digital evidence. And for that reason, because there are a lot of —in laboratories it is accredited, but outside of laboratories it is not accredited. There is no chain of custody, there are no policy and procedures, there are no technical review and administrative review of reports. So, for me, it would be digital evidence.

Mr. TSIN-A-TSOI. I concur with my colleagues.

In general, perhaps, it is the areas in which the human being becomes the measuring instrument himself, operating from the database from in his brain that has not been published publicly, which means that every human being might have a different opinion.

Senator BLUMENTHAL. Well, again, I want to thank you all. Obviously, there is a lot of work to be done in this area.

Again, my thanks to the Chairman.

And thank you also to the excellent staff work that was done for this committee hearing. And I know that we received an excellent memo from the staff in preparation for it, so I want to thank them as well.

Thank you, Mr. Chairman.

The CHAIRMAN. Thank you, Senator.

It has been a very interesting hearing. I am going to close with something from the book. And I didn't get to ask any of the questions that I wanted to ask.

[Laughter.]

The CHAIRMAN. But that is OK, because, I mean, this is a hard subject. And I will send those questions.

But it is a hard subject, and it has to be broached, and it is not one which is easily discussed.

But from page 23 of this book, that is, the "Strengthening Forensic Science in the United States: A Path Forward," which was put out, the following is said. And this obviously I agree with, so understand that.

"Scientific and medical assessment conducted in forensic investigation should be independent of law enforcement efforts either to prosecute criminal suspects or even to determine whether a criminal act has indeed been committed. The best science is conducted in a scientific setting as opposed to a law enforcement setting. Because forensic scientists often are driven in their work by a need to answer a particular question related to the issues of a particular case, they sometimes feel pressure to sacrifice appropriate methodology for the sake of expediency."

That comports with some stuff that I have watched and looked at. It doesn't necessarily tell the story of anything in particular.

I think this has been a very, very good hearing even though you are probably all somewhat aghast.

[Laughter.]

The CHAIRMAN. But so be it. It is an important subject. If it is hard to approach, then so be that. We have to continue at this, and we will.

So I very much appreciate all of you being here.

And this hearing is adjourned.

[Whereupon, at 4:25 p.m., the hearing was adjourned.]

APPENDIX

RESPONSE TO WRITTEN QUESTIONS SUBMITTED BY HON. JOHN D. ROCKEFELLER IV TO DR. T. (TJARK) TJIN-A-TSOI

Question 1. The Netherlands Forensic Institute (NFI) not only serves law enforcement needs but also acts as a "high-tech knowledge hub." Research and development are an integral part of its mission. How has NFI integrated research and development into its work?

Answer. The essence of the business model of NFI, is that it considers itself to be an independent provider of forensic products and services to law enforcement (police, prosecution, magristrates) and all other relevant governmental and intergovernmental customers.

In this approach innovation of products and services through research and development (R&D) is an integral part of the business model of the NFI. This is similar to the way private technology firms operate when they conduct R&D and innovate in order to create unique value for their customers.

In other words, even though NFI is government owned and not-for-profit, it has adopted some of the basic concepts and organizational structures from the private sector aiming at becoming a highly innovative and efficient provider of forensic products and services.

Consequently, R&D within the NFI is managed in more or less the same way as it is in the private sector. R&D costs are part of the integral cost base of the product (groups).

In some departments, there are dedicated R&D units. In other departments R&D is conducted part time by scientists that also do casework.

Whenever possible, R&D projects are structured as "co-creation" projects, which means in essence that the customers are highly involved in order to make sure highly valuable innovations are created and wasteful expenditures are avoided.

In the context of R&D the NFI has adopted an open innovation approach in which public private partnerships and consortia with academia have been developed.

Question 2. The National Forensics Institute has been able to get rid of backlogs and even shorten the time needed to analyze evidence. Five years ago, its average delivery time was 140 days, while today it is about 13 days. What reforms were implemented to eliminate backlogs and long turnaround times?

Answer. The measures that the Netherlands Forensic Institute (NFI) took to eliminate its backlog and reduce delivery times are described in detail in the whitepaper "Trends, challenges and strategy in the forensic science sector" by the NFI CEO Dr. T. Tjin-A-Tsoi.

In essence there were three main developments:

- implementing a new business model which involved a more businesslike approach towards are customers and "negotiating" a Service Level Agreement with them;
- redesigning operational (production) processes in order to make them more efficient and less time consuming;
- redirecting the R&D effort towards innovative technical methods for faster delivery.

To a certain extent all three developments involved changing the organizational culture. As this is always the most difficult thing to achieve, especially when the culture has been around for quite a while—like in the forensic community—strong commitment and strong leadership by senior management was essential.

No additional funds were made available to the NFI in order to combat the backlogs.

As experiences around the world—and economic theory—have shown, backlogs are an inevitable consequence of the technology driven growth in the demand for forensic services, combined with the way crime labs are usually funded. Most crime labs receive a fixed annual budget, without having agreements with its customers on the amount of forensic investigations that can be delivered, given those resources. The officers actually commissioning the forensic investigations are not aware of the costs of these investigations and have no idea which part of total capacity their investigation will consume. This problem can be solved in several ways, but a relatively low-impact method is to get all parties to agree to a service level agreement (SLA) and to put in place mechanisms to make sure supply and demand are not completely out of balance.

Question 3. Thanks to the National Academies report on forensic science, we know that many forensic methods lack scientific reliability and may have unacceptably high error rates. To what extent can we trust the results of forensic tests that have not yet been rigorously and independently tested?

Answer. It is difficult to make a general statement on this subject. When a solid scientific basis is lacking, quality and reliability may vary from one lab to another, and even from one practitioner to another. Subjective personal opinions of forensic examiners become a substitute for objective scientific knowledge based on empirical research. For decades these opinions went unquestioned. The supposed scientific authority of forensic practitioners became a source of pride for practitioners and a convenient instrument for law enforcement and courts.

Police officers, prosecutors and even judges tend to push forensic practitioners to give clear "yes or no" answers, even when this is impossible. There are clear examples of cases and even whole forensic disciplines in which this tendency was accommodated, even though it cannot be justified scientifically.

What is needed is empirical scientific research in order to create a solid scientific basis and scientific standards. However, this will require a different culture and structure in the forensic community. At the moment the forensic sector is highly fragmented and crime labs are often relatively small production units that do not have the resources to conduct R&D. Furthermore, crime labs are often part of police organisations and become infused with police culture, with its specific operational pressures. This is not necessarily conducive to independent scientific development.

With this in mind, the NFI has developed a dedicated empirical science program with respect to 'objective interpretation' within all its forensic disciplines.

RESPONSE TO WRITTEN QUESTIONS SUBMITTED BY HON. MARK WARNER TO DR. T. (TJARK) TJIN-A-TSOI

Question 1. Currently, public labs must re-check any forensic testing and results that are outsourced to private labs. However, the cost of analyzing DNA samples in private laboratories can be up to 50 percent less than the cost of comparable analyses conducted by public laboratories, due to private investments in R&D to lower costs and remain competitive.

Do you think that a partnership between public and private labs would be beneficial? Could it help to reduce pressure on public labs in instances when there is a higher demand for analysis? If you disagree, please explain why.

Answer. It is questionable whether handling only the overflow of public labs is a viable business model for private labs, because the overflow is highly volatile. Private companies would probably require a more steady contractual relationship, which leads to the fundamental question whether forensic examinations are intrinsically a government activity. This is a political question. Nevertheless, it is possible to outsource some of the work to private labs and I see no reason why this should lead to poor quality, given the experience in other sectors in which quality control is essential. However, outsourcing to the private sector is not for free. An obvious alternative is to spend the same funds to increase the capacity of existing public labs, giving them more mass and thus capturing economies of scale. It is in that sense interesting that there is reluctance to work with demand driven funding structures ("pay for service") in case of public labs, whereas there seems to be no problem when the same customer (law enforcement agency) works with private labs. In both cases public money is being spent.

Question 2. If there is a partnership, should private labs have direct access to the Combined DNA Index System (CODIS)? If not, please explain why.

Answer. Witness chose not to respond.

Question 3. No data currently exists on private vs. public lab rates of error in analysis. Do you believe it would be beneficial to have an independent evaluation of this data? If not, please explain why.

Answer. Witness chose not to respond.

Question 4. All CODIS labs must be accredited and audited annually, and analysts are required to undergo semiannual professional testing—However, this only applies to DNA analyses, not any other types of forensic analyses (ballistics testing, fingerprint testing, toxicology, etc.)

One of the possible solutions would be to require accreditation and other types of quality control, such as proficiency testing of analysts and blind review or auditing of actual casework to be sure it satisfies defined standards.

What is the best way to establish a consistent accreditation and quality control process? Should a Federal entity handle this work, rather than private entities? If not, please explain why.

Answer. Witness chose not to respond.

Question 5. Why hasn't voluntary accreditation by private entities involved proficiency testing of analysts or routine auditing of casework?

Answer. Witness chose not to respond.

Question 6. Should recipients of Federal funding be required to maintain quality controls, such as routine proficiency testing, blind review of casework, and certification that an independent entity will perform external investigations into possible misconduct? If not, please explain why not.

Answer. Witness chose not to respond.

Question 7. One of the key findings in the 2009 National Academies report—Strengthening Forensic Science in the U.S.: A Path Forward—concluded that the forensic science community is hampered "in the sense that it has only thin ties to an academic research base that could support the forensic science disciplines and fill knowledge gaps." The report also noted that "adding more dollars and people to the enterprise might reduce case backlogs, but it will not address fundamental limitations in the capabilities of forensic science disciplines to discern valued information from crime scene evidence."

Further, the report concluded that "funding for academic research is limited and requires law enforcement collaboration, which can inhibit the pursuit of more fundamental scientific questions essential to establishing the foundation of forensic science." Does the current Congressional approach address this problem sufficiently? Is there anything else we can do to reduce barriers and further forensic research?

Answer. I agree with the statement that the forensic community is hampered in the sense that there is not enough scientific research and innovation, and that the community has only thin ties to an academic research base. However, before additional money is spent, I believe it is important to be clear about the root causes of the present situation.

One root cause is the lack of supply and demand coordination, which has led to persistent backlog problems. Backlogs tend to drown out other activities, like R&D. All additional funds tend to be used to combat the backlog problem. Solving this problem is, therefore, a critical step towards solving other problems in the forensic community.

Another root cause is the fragmentation of the forensic sector, in the sense that it consists of many, relatively small, and separate production units that operate for the benefit (and inside) of local police organizations and jurisdictions. These units lack the critical mass that is needed to conduct expensive R&D programs. Furthermore, the culture and specific operational pressures of police organizations are not necessarily the ideal organizational context for scientific development and innovation. Most government crime labs in the US, or indeed around the world, are relatively small and not independent organizations. This is certainly one of the root causes of the problem. (The Netherlands Forensic Institute is an independent government agency, which is definitely one of the main reasons why it has consistently been able to allocate substantial resources to R&D and innovation.)

A third root cause is that crime labs that do want to use proprietary funds to invest in R&D often have to do this without financial contributions of other labs. The reason for this is that in the forensic sector it is more or less common practice, that scientific and technological results of proprietary R&D efforts are given away to other government labs free of charge. Although this may look like beneficial fraternal behavior between government entities, it actually leads to a dearth of R&D. There is no financial incentive to invest in R&D if all the financial risks are to be borne by the lab carrying out the R&D, while all the outcomes are shared free of charge. This type of free rider behavior is detrimental to R&D in the long run. R&D programs thus tend to become completely dependent on individual grants, which lack the continuity for persistent scientific development over a number of years or even decades.

It is sometimes argued that the lack of R&D could be solved by creating a centralized system of R&D-oriented institutes, possibly universities or other research institutions. These would then perform most of the research, while the casework would be done by the existing system of local crime labs. The theory is that this research would subsequently 'diffuse' into the forensic system. There are reasons to be highly skeptical about this approach, as it would not address the aforementioned root causes. It would be similar to a world in which companies do not carry out R&D, but only use what universities and other research institutions come up with. Experience has shown that a severe disconnect is likely to arise between the central research institutes and the hundreds of separately managed production units doing all the case work. After all, even integrated technology companies often struggle to keep their R&D programs in line with the needs of the customers, or to implement innovations throughout the organization. If casework and R&D are separated, the probable outcome will be research that is very clever, but that not necessarily reflects what the customers want or need. In other words, there is a need for basic research that could partially be carried out by R&D-centers, but this cannot replace the need for customer oriented R&D by forensic service providers (crime labs) themselves. This means that the aforementioned root causes should be addressed.

Question 8. When I was governor of Virginia, I ordered DNA testing on all cases in 2004 in which biological evidence was preserved, but no DNA testing was done because the technique was not available at the time. This review resulted in a number of exonerations and I am very proud of VA's role in securing the freedom of these innocent people. When the testing process was done, I was made aware of delays by the Virginia Department of Forensic Science in notifying individuals in whose cases the DNA did not match the evidence in their case file.

What processes are in place to notify people when there is evidence of innocence? As we fund research on forensic science, if a technique like bite mark identification is found to be unreliable or if firearms identification testimony is found to be beyond the limits of science, what processes are in place in crime labs or elsewhere in the criminal justice system to make sure that people with relevant cases aren't kept in the dark?

Answer. Witness chose not to respond.

Question 9. Should Congress require states to submit data on crime lab backlogs as a requisite for receiving Federal grant funding? If not, please explain why.

Answer. Witness chose not to respond.

Question 10. Does the Bureau of Justice Statistics (BJS) survey of public crime labs require states to assess their backlogs? If not, would this be an appropriate requirement?

Answer. Witness chose not to respond.

RESPONSE TO WRITTEN QUESTIONS SUBMITTED BY HON. JOHN D. ROCKEFELLER IV TO MICHAEL R. BROMWICH

Question 1. The National Academy of Sciences recommended that Congress create a new Federal agency to conduct rigorous, independent research and testing in the forensic sciences. If that isn't possible in the current budget climate, what other steps can Congress take to improve the science underpinning forensic techniques?

Answer. If creating a new Federal agency is not possible, Congress can take other steps to ensure that the major steps identified by the National Academy of Sciences to improve the delivery of forensic science services are assigned to Federal agencies that have the relevant expertise. Basic and applied scientific research grants for forensic disciplines should be funded by the National Science Foundation (NSF), and measurement standards and other best practices and standards should be developed and established by the National Institute of Standards and Technology (NIST). The Department of Justice (DOJ) can and should play an important role in ensuring implementation of those best practices and standards, accreditation of laboratories, and certification of forensic practitioners. Adherence to established standards, practices, and quality measures can be tied to Federal grants supporting forensic science such as the Coverdell and DNA Backlog Reduction grants.

Question 2. As a former Federal prosecutor, what advice and precautions would you give prosecutors who are using forensic evidence in trying cases?

Answer. Prosecutors who makes use of forensic evidence in their cases should realize that such evidence can be a powerful tool to convict the guilty and exonerate the innocent. Because of its great power, forensic evidence should be analyzed critically by prosecutors and not accepted as revealed truth simply because an expert witness provides it. Too often, that has been the case in the past. We have seen too many cases in which passive prosecutors failed to make any inquiry at all into the factual and scientific bases of an expert's findings, which has led in many cases to flawed analysis, misleading testimony, and erroneous convictions. At a very basic level, prosecutors should make themselves aware of the very real issues associated with certain forensic disciplines, which have thus far not shown themselves able to conclusively link evidence to specific individuals, and which therefore limits the probative value of expert scientific testimony. Prosecutors should be wary about expert forensic testimony that relies on anecdotal experience to imply uniqueness—that is what many of the examiners did in the cases we reviewed in the Department of Justice Office of the Inspector General's investigation of the FBI Laboratory. *http://www.justice.gov/oig/special/9704a/index.htm.* Furthermore, not only is it the duty of prosecutors to ensure that the experts they are proffering testify in ways that are fully scientifically defensible, but the prosecutor must also take care not to overstate the strength of forensic findings in arguments to the jury.

RESPONSE TO WRITTEN QUESTION SUBMITTED BY HON. AMY KLOBUCHAR TO MICHAEL R. BROMWICH

Question. Whether it's the popularity of TV shows such as CSI or simply young people's interest in science and desire for public service, there has been an increasing awareness of Forensic Science as a career path. I've worked to encourage efforts to link employers with two and four year colleges to increase practical STEM training for workers. How would developing standards of accreditation for forensic training programs and degrees help make it easier for students to find work in the field and to improve the quality of our forensic labs?

Answer. National standards would help ensure that forensic training programs and academic degree programs provide the education, training, experience, and technical skills to give forensic labs the personnel they need. Such standards would promote confidence that the personnel being hired are qualified to perform the work performed in those labs. Incoming employees who are the products of accredited forensic training programs would require less time to be spent at the outset of their employment on basic training. Graduates of such programs would offer improved technical skills for professional forensic practice, and would deepen the scientific resources of the laboratory. All that being said, the biggest problem facing aspiring forensic scientists is the budget crunch faced by virtually all public forensic labs.

RESPONSE TO WRITTEN QUESTIONS SUBMITTED BY HON. MARK WARNER TO MICHAEL R. BROMWICH

Question 1. Currently, public labs must re-check any forensic testing and results that are outsourced to private labs. However, the cost of analyzing DNA samples in private laboratories can be up to 50 percent less than the cost of comparable analyses conducted by public laboratories, due to private investments in R&D to lower costs and remain competitive.

Do you think that a partnership between public and private labs would be beneficial? Could it help to reduce pressure on public labs in instances when there is a higher demand for analysis? If you disagree, please explain why.

Answer. Partnerships between public and private labs could result in an improvement in service to the criminal justice system. Private labs could help alleviate backlogs for public laboratories, and well-funded private labs may have more sophisticated equipment and deeper scientific resources. A public-private partnership could allow the public labs to take advantage of equipment, training, and other intellectual resources the private laboratory can offer. I should add that I view such a partnership as a necessary evil rather than a desirable state of affairs. I think forensic analysis conducted in local, state and Federal criminal justice systems is an inherently governmental function—indeed a core function of government. It is shameful that our criminal justice system should have to rely on private resources of any kind to support inherent governmental functions, but unfortunately this has become a necessity in some jurisdictions.

Question 2. If there is a partnership, should private labs have direct access to the Combined DNA Index System (CODIS)? If not, please explain why.

Answer. I do not know enough about the merits of the issue to offer an informed opinion.

Question 3. No data currently exists on private vs. public lab rates of error in analysis. Do you believe it would be beneficial to have an independent evaluation of this data? If not, please explain why.

Answer. I am not sure what purpose would be served by collecting such data. I assume it would show that better funded private laboratories, with more skilled, more highly compensated personnel, better equipment, and better training, make fewer errors. Those would be a wholly unsurprising result. It would simply underscore the need to provide better funding for public laboratories, not that we would be better off offloading more forensic analysis to private labs.

Question 4. All CODIS labs must be accredited and audited annually, and analysts are required to undergo semiannual professional testing—However, this only applies to DNA analyses, not any other types of forensic analyses (ballistics testing, fingerprint testing, toxicology, etc.)

One of the possible solutions would be to require accreditation and other types of quality control, such as proficiency testing of analysts and blind review or auditing of actual casework to be sure it satisfies defined standards.

What is the best way to establish a consistent accreditation and quality control process? Should a Federal entity handle this work, rather than private entities? If not, please explain why.

Answer. The National Institute of Standards and Technology (NIST) is a Federal agency that can play an important role in establishing a consistent accreditation and quality control process that harmonizes the practice of laboratories across the country. To promote uniformity and adherence to the highest standards, NIST should play a coordinating and standards development role.

Question 5. Why hasn't voluntary accreditation by private entities involved proficiency testing of analysts or routine auditing of casework?

Answer. Voluntary accreditation of forensic laboratories by private entities does involve requirements for the administration of proficiency testing and auditing of casework, but there is much room for improvement. Most forensic practitioners do not need to complete an external proficiency test on an annual basis. Forensic proficiency tests can be improved by double-blind administration and should be designed to mirror casework as much as possible. Casework is audited during accreditation on-site surveillance visits, but analysts are allowed in many cases to select files for the auditors to review. To improve audits of casework, casework should be selected by the auditor at random and at least some surveillance visits should take place unannounced.

Question 6. Should recipients of Federal funding be required to maintain quality controls, such as routine proficiency testing, blind review of casework, and certification that an independent entity will perform external investigations into possible misconduct? If not, please explain why not.

Answer. Maintaining quality controls, including those described in the question, should be a minimum standard for all forensic laboratories. Recipients of Federal funding should be required to meet these criteria, because the Federal Government should not aid and abet inferior and flawed forensic analysis. Currently, the Paul Coverdell Forensic Science Improvement Grants Program awards grants to states and units of local government to help improve the quality and timeliness of forensic science and medical examiner services. The Coverdell Grant program requires that a grant applicant certify that an external, independent entity is available to conduct investigations into allegations of serious negligence or misconduct.

Question 7. One of the key findings in the 2009 National Academies report—Strengthening Forensic Science in the U.S.: A Path Forward—concluded that the forensic science community is hampered "in the sense that it has only thin ties to an academic research base that could support the forensic science disciplines and fill knowledge gaps." The report also noted that "adding more dollars and people to the enterprise might reduce case backlogs, but it will not address fundamental limitations in the capabilities of forensic science disciplines to discern valued information from crime scene evidence."

Further, the report concluded that "funding for academic research is limited and requires law enforcement collaboration, which can inhibit the pursuit of more fundamental scientific questions essential to establishing the foundation of forensic science." Does the current Congressional approach address this problem sufficiently? Is there anything else we can do to reduce barriers and further forensic research?

Answer. Congress has an opportunity to expand academic research in forensic science and to raise the level of research in this field. To date, it has not done so. In the past, law enforcement entities, primarily the Department of Justice, have been the only agencies funding forensic science research. The interests of law enforcement may not always align with the most pressing research needs, including those that might call into question or undermine categories of forensic analysis widely used by prosecutors. By funding forensic science research through grants to science agencies such as the National Science Foundation (NSF), Congress can ensure that the highest scientific standards are met and that the research will be conducted independently.

The concern that law enforcement backing could create barriers to conducting basic scientific research in the forensic sciences is real and is based on the history of forensic science funding. Congress could improve that system by ensuring that law enforcement agencies are not the sole arbiters of worthy forensic science research.

Question 8. When I was governor of Virginia, I ordered DNA testing on all cases in 2004 in which biological evidence was preserved, but no DNA testing was done because the technique was not available at the time. This review resulted in a number of exonerations and I am very proud of VA's role in securing the freedom of these innocent people. When the testing process was done, I was made aware of delays by the Virginia Department of Forensic Science in notifying individuals in whose cases the DNA did not match the evidence in their case file.

What processes are in place to notify people when there is evidence of innocence? As we fund research on forensic science, if a technique like bite mark identification is found to be unreliable or if firearms identification testimony is found to be beyond the limits of science, what processes are in place in crime labs or elsewhere in the criminal justice system to make sure that people with relevant cases aren't kept in the dark?

Answer. At present, there are no model systems in place to notify defendants in those instances when negligence, misconduct, or flawed science is found to have affected criminal cases. The problem of defendant notification has multiple challenges: (1) Identification of defendants in whose cases the faulty evidence was involved, (2) Notification of affected defendants, who may or may not be in prison, and (3) Legal representation for those defendants, many of whom are indigent. The current FBI Hair Review has created an opportunity to address these fundamental and important issues and create processes for defendant notification. All states and localities should create a defendant notification system that clearly assigns participants in the criminal justice system appropriate roles and responsibilities. The lessons learned from the current FBI hair review and the many other state-level attempts to right the wrongs of faulty forensic analysis should provide a foundation for developing a coherent and effective defendant notification policy.

Question 9. Should Congress require states to submit data on crime lab backlogs as a requisite for receiving Federal grant funding? If not, please explain why.

Answer. Yes. Such data would be worthwhile, but for the data to be meaningful, a uniform definition of backlog would need to be employed. Without more, mere backlog numbers would not be particularly informative.

Even more important than the backlog numbers themselves is an analysis of why some states experience substantial backlogs and others do not. By learning why backlogs occur in some jurisdictions but not in others, guidance could be provided to help state criminal justice systems manage their demand v. resource challenges.

Question 10. Does the Bureau of Justice Statistics (BJS) survey of public crime labs require states to assess their backlogs? If not, would this be an appropriate requirement?

Answer. In the 2009 Census of Publicly Funded Forensic Crime Laboratories,[1] the BJS reports the numbers of backlogs, but not backlog numbers by state. Reporting the numbers of backlogged cases by state would provide members of Congress and state legislatures with important data that would be useful in making funding and policy decisions.

RESPONSE TO WRITTEN QUESTIONS SUBMITTED BY HON. JOHN D. ROCKEFELLER IV TO DR. GREGORY A. SCHMUNK

Question 1. The National Academy of Sciences recommended that Congress create a new Federal agency to conduct rigorous, independent research and testing in the forensic sciences. If that isn't possible in the current budget climate, what other steps can Congress take to improve the science underpinning forensic techniques?

Answer. The National Association of Medical Examiners (NAME) strongly supports the NAS recommendation for a new Federal agency (National Institute of Forensic Science-NIFS) to achieve these goals and sees it as the foundation for the remainder of the NRC recommendations. But NAME also recognizes that there might be impediments to establishing such a new agency at this time. If a new and independent agency is unattainable at present, NAME believes that the duties of such an agency should be placed, as a bridging step, into a new Office of Forensic Services (OFS) within an existing agency fulfilling the spirit of the NRC recommendations.

[1] See: *http://www.bjs.gov/content/pub/pdf/cpffcl09.pdf* (last accessed August 28, 2013)

An OFS could be established with relative structural independence from its parent agency. This is primarily achieved by placing the decision-making power in a committee of experts from the community, rather than the bureaucracy of the parent agency. Thus, if an OFS is placed within DOJ, the final decision-making should not be by the Attorney General. One strategy to accomplish this separation of power is to have advisory committees develop recommendations and an oversight committee accept or reject the recommendations—sending forward accepted recommendations, but sending rejected recommendations back to the advisory committee for revision. Although stakeholders such as prosecutors and law enforcement officials should have input into the process, the decision-making should be primarily from researchers and practitioners. NAME believes that NIST and the CDC have scientific expertise that would make their participation useful. NAME also believes that transparency and community input must be part of the regulatory oversight.

Independence of research and testing is best accomplished through grants to independent academic institutions, rather than by Federal institutions themselves which might have conflicts of interest. Some grants could build "Center" type capacity in a few institutions in order to achieve a critical mass of investigators capable of multidisciplinary studies. However, other grants should go to academic institutions with an interest in building forensic science and forensic medicine research in collaboration with forensic practitioners.

The NAS report outlines that one of the functions of NIFS is to establish and enforce best practices for forensic science professionals. In the arena of medico-legal death investigation, NAME has established Forensic Autopsy Performance Standards as well as an Inspection and Accreditation program that can be used for this purpose.

NAME believes that an essential function of NIFS or an OFS would be to conduct periodic forensic science needs assessments at the federal, state, regional, and local levels in order to ensure optimal provision of resources to service providers. Such assessments should also consider research needs. The assessment results should be presented in a report.

Question 2. According to a recent poll of National Association of Medical Examiners (NAME) members, 70 percent of medical examiners have been pressured to reach a particular conclusion. Is it this kind of political pressure that has prompted NAME to call for greater independence from law enforcement?

Answer. NAME is strongly supportive of the independence of the Medicolegal Death Investigation system from the influence of law enforcement and other criminal justice agencies as was recommended by the NAS report. Pressures on forensic pathologists in the course of their duties can come from many other sources. Pressures may come from families who are upset that a ruling on manner of death is suicide. Pressures may come from government officials who may disagree with the medico-legal conclusions that are contrary to their interests. Prosecutorial bias is among the more important and pernicious concerns, and NAME believes that medico-legal death investigation offices should not be under law enforcement agencies, but rather should appear independent and be independent. NAME is, at the most basic level, supportive of a system which considers neutral, objective, and evidence based scientific data in reaching conclusions on cause and manner of death. As the popular television programs state, we simply need to "follow the evidence" in reaching our conclusions. The public needs to be confident that our conclusions are based upon such evidence and are free of any conflict of interest. This may be most apparent in reaching conclusions in law enforcement-related or in-custody deaths, but a similar need to be free of conflict exists where the family may suffer distress or financial hardship (such as denial of insurance benefits) with determinations such as suicide. It should be kept in mind that all professional groups, including NAME, the American Medical Association, the College of American Pathologists, and the American Society of Clinical Pathologists to name a few, strongly consider that the determination of cause and manner of death is a medical decision, to be decided by medical professionals. In the medico-legal environment these determinations should be the realm of Forensic Pathologists and Medical Examiners. In the same way that no person would ever conceive of delegating their clinical diagnosis and medical care to someone other than a professional specifically trained in the medical field that was relevant to their illness or injury, so should political entities and the public demand and be assured that a medical professional specifically trained in forensic medicine and the determination of cause and manner of death is making the medico-legal diagnoses and determinations of cause and manner of death. NAME believes that all medico-legal death investigative offices should be headed by a forensic pathologist, rather than by coroners or administrators which have a greater propensity to politicization and significantly lesser backgrounds in science and forensic medicine.

Question 3. Thanks to the National Academies report on forensic science, we know that many forensic methods lack scientific reliability and may have unacceptably high error rates. To what extent can we trust the results of forensic tests that have not yet been rigorously and independently tested?

Answer. Research is the platform upon which all of forensic science stands. NAME strongly supports increased basic science and applied research. Research provides the answer to the question of error rates. Additional research must be undertaken to refine the practice of forensic pathology, including better understanding of the error rates applicable to this discipline. With this goal in mind, it is important to foster and support increased collaboration between the many practitioners of forensic pathology, largely based in states and counties, with researchers based in academic programs. Academic centers have research assets including trained investigators, laboratories, and administrative and compliance support for sponsored projects. However, these academic institutions oftentimes need practicing forensic scientists and pathologists who can ensure that research projects are focused on relevant questions and participate in multidisciplinary approaches to complex forensic issues.

RESPONSE TO WRITTEN QUESTION SUBMITTED BY HON. AMY KLOBUCHAR TO DR. GREGORY A. SCHMUNK

Question. Whether it's the popularity of TV shows such as CSI or simply young people's interest in science and desire for public service, there has been an increasing awareness of Forensic Science as a career path. I've worked to encourage efforts to link employers with two and four year colleges to increase practical STEM training for workers. How would developing standards of accreditation for forensic training programs and degrees help make it easier for students to find work in the field and to improve the quality of our forensic labs?

Answer. There is currently a national shortage of forensic pathologists as identified in the recent report, "Increasing the Supply of Forensic Pathologists in the United States: A Report and Recommendations", from the National Institute of Justice sponsored Scientific Working Group for Medicolegal Death Investigation (SWGMDI). We are simply not graduating enough forensic pathologists to meet the needs of the country, especially if it is the desire of the Federal Government to improve the overall quality of forensic pathology services in the nation, and not just accept excellence in only some states and counties, leaving other elements of the population (frequently rural or sparsely populated areas) to endure substandard services. This shortage mirrors the more global issue of shortage in Graduate Medical Education positions as a whole in the country. Over 500 medical school graduates were unable to find *any* residency program in the past year. Despite the existence of 113 medical schools in the U.S. there are only 37 accredited forensic pathology programs. Salaries for forensic pathologists and trainees are lower than for other disciplines in pathology, discouraging medical students from becoming forensic pathologists. Forensic pathology residency programs are the only subspecialty of medicine not subsidized by the Federal Government, as they are not hospital based. Increased funding of academic pathology residency programs could create partnerships with medical examiner offices to provide enhanced training and research opportunities for forensic pathology residents and address our national manpower shortage in this discipline. Training programs in forensic pathology need increased funding to supply the pathologists necessary for the Nation's work to be done.

Forensic pathology has a long established program for certification and accreditation. The Accreditation Council for Graduate Medical Education (ACGME) has accredited forensic pathology training programs since 1982. This process replaced a previous accreditation program administered by the American Medical Association (AMA) Council on Medical Education in conjunction with the American Board of Pathology (ABP) which had been in place since 1961.

The ABP has certified individual forensic pathologists since 1959. As physicians, all forensic pathologists are licensed and required to complete regular continuing education requirements to maintain their license. Additional requirements for Maintenance of Certification (MOC) have been instituted by the ABP in order to maintain subspecialty certifications.

NAME has accredited Medicolegal Death Investigation offices since 1974 and has had professional standards for autopsy performance since 2005.

The American Board of Medicolegal Death Investigation (ABMDI) has certified Medicolegal Death Investigators since 1998.

These clear and well established paths to accreditation and certification exist in all aspects of Medicolegal Death Investigation and have been accepted for many years by the Federal Government. This represents an excellent model for what the Federal Government might wish to achieve with regard to accreditation and certification in other forensic science disciplines.

However, major areas which still need to be addressed are developing a qualified pool of practitioners to enter the field including creating incentives for individuals to choose death investigation as a career, and creating incentives for state and county governments to ensure that their death investigation offices are accredited. Federal support as outlined in my presentation will assist in all of these areas.

RESPONSE TO WRITTEN QUESTIONS SUBMITTED BY HON. MARK WARNER TO DR. GREGORY A. SCHMUNK

Question 1. Currently, public labs must re-check any forensic testing and results that are outsourced to private labs. However, the cost of analyzing DNA samples in private laboratories can be up to 50 percent less than the cost of comparable analyses conducted by public laboratories, due to private investments in R&D to lower costs and remain competitive.

Do you think that a partnership between public and private labs would be beneficial? Could it help to reduce pressure on public labs in instances when there is a higher demand for analysis? If you disagree, please explain why.

Answer. NAME feels that these questions are applicable to crime labs and therefore would defer remarks to experts in that field.

Question 2. If there is a partnership, should private labs have direct access to the Combined DNA Index System (CODIS)? If not, please explain why.

Answer. NAME feels that these questions are applicable to crime labs and therefore would defer remarks to experts in that field.

Question 3. No data currently exists on private vs. public lab rates of error in analysis. Do you believe it would be beneficial to have an independent evaluation of this data? If not, please explain why.

Answer. NAME feels that these questions are applicable to crime labs and therefore would defer remarks to experts in that field.

Question 4. All CODIS labs must be accredited and audited annually, and analysts are required to undergo semiannual professional testing—However, this only applies to DNA analyses, not any other types of forensic analyses (ballistics testing, fingerprint testing, toxicology, etc.)

One of the possible solutions would be to require accreditation and other types of quality control, such as proficiency testing of analysts and blind review or auditing of actual casework to be sure it satisfies defined standards.

What is the best way to establish a consistent accreditation and quality control process? Should a Federal entity handle this work, rather than private entities? If not, please explain why.

Answer. NAME agrees that proper quality assurance (QA) programs are essential to ensuring that the product of laboratories is of the highest quality. NAME has incorporated multiple QA requirements into our Inspection and Accreditation process. The American Board of Pathology, state medical licensure boards and the American Board of Medicolegal Death Investigation all require documentation of continuing education on a regular basis. Proficiency testing is one component of quality assurance. The NAME Inspection and Accreditation standards require regular participation in established QA programs such as the American Society of Clinical Pathology (ASCP) Case Reports (formerly Check Sample) program. We also require review of casework via a defined process. NAME favors Federal funding being tied to documentation of ongoing QA programs.

NAME also recognizes that oversight is essential within the medico-legal death investigative system. A citizen must have a proper avenue by which to address complaints. Several states, such as Maryland, have procedures for appeal defined in state statute. This answer was more fully explored in the answer to Chairman Rockefeller's second question.

Question 5. Why hasn't voluntary accreditation by private entities involved proficiency testing of analysts or routine auditing of casework?

Answer. NAME agrees that proper quality assurance (QA) programs are essential to ensuring that the product of laboratories is of the highest quality. NAME has incorporated multiple QA requirements into our Inspection and Accreditation process. The American Board of Pathology, state medical licensure boards and the American Board of Medicolegal Death Investigation all require documentation of continuing education on a regular basis. Proficiency testing is one component of quality assurance. The NAME Inspection and Accreditation standards require regular participation in established QA programs such as the American Society of Clinical Pathology (ASCP) Case Reports (formerly Check Sample) program. We also require review of casework via a defined process. NAME favors Federal funding being tied to documentation of ongoing QA programs. NAME also recognizes that oversight is essential within the medico-legal death investigative system. A citizen must have a proper avenue by which to address complaints. Several states, such as Maryland, have procedures for appeal defined in state statute. This answer was more fully explored in the answer to Chairman Rockefeller's second question.

Question 6. Should recipients of Federal funding be required to maintain quality controls, such as routine proficiency testing, blind review of casework, and certification that an independent entity will perform external investigations into possible misconduct? If not, please explain why not.

Answer. NAME agrees that proper quality assurance (QA) programs are essential to ensuring that the product of laboratories is of the highest quality. NAME has incorporated multiple QA requirements into our Inspection and Accreditation process. The American Board of Pathology, state medical licensure boards and the American Board of Medicolegal Death Investigation all require documentation of continuing education on a regular basis. Proficiency testing is one component of quality assurance. The NAME Inspection and Accreditation standards require regular participation in established QA programs such as the American Society of Clinical Pathology (ASCP) Case Reports (formerly Check Sample) program. We also require review of casework via a defined process. NAME favors Federal funding being tied to documentation of ongoing QA programs. NAME also recognizes that oversight is essential within the medico-legal death investigative system. A citizen must have a proper avenue by which to address complaints. Several states, such as Maryland, have procedures for appeal defined in state statute. This answer was more fully explored in the answer to Chairman Rockefeller's second question.

Question 7. One of the key findings in the 2009 National Academies report—Strengthening Forensic Science in the U.S.: A Path Forward—concluded that the forensic science community is hampered "in the sense that it has only thin ties to an academic research base that could support the forensic science disciplines and fill knowledge gaps." The report also noted that "adding more dollars and people to the enterprise might reduce case backlogs, but it will not address fundamental limitations in the capabilities of forensic science disciplines to discern valued information from crime scene evidence."

Further, the report concluded that "funding for academic research is limited and requires law enforcement collaboration, which can inhibit the pursuit of more fundamental scientific questions essential to establishing the foundation of forensic science." Does the current Congressional approach address this problem sufficiently? Is there anything else we can do to reduce barriers and further forensic research?

Answer. NAME strongly advocates both basic and applied grant supported research in the forensic sciences. It is our impression that the CDC and NIJ do not adequately see forensic pathology as a discipline deserving basic research support. Furthermore, forensic pathology practitioners are not usually housed in academic institutions, and academic centers usually do not interact with their local forensic pathologists. It is important to bring these two groups together to foster research. Another logistical problem is that most forensic pathologists are fully occupied with their daily workload and do not have time for research projects. State and county agencies providing funding to medico-legal death investigation offices rarely perceive the value of research by forensic pathologists. CDC, NIJ, NIH and other Federal agencies should create mentoring, pilot and career development awards and grants to foster practitioner-based research.

Question 8. When I was governor of Virginia, I ordered DNA testing on all cases in 2004 in which biological evidence was preserved, but no DNA testing was done because the technique was not available at the time. This review resulted in a number of exonerations and I am very proud of VA's role in securing the freedom of these innocent people. When the testing process was done, I was made aware of delays by the Virginia Department of Forensic Science in notifying individuals in whose cases the DNA did not match the evidence in their case file.

What processes are in place to notify people when there is evidence of innocence? As we fund research on forensic science, if a technique like bite mark identification is found to be unreliable or if firearms identification testimony is found to be beyond the limits of science, what processes are in place in crime labs or elsewhere in the criminal justice system to make sure that people with relevant cases aren't kept in the dark?

Answer. NAME agrees that procedures need to be in place to notify the proper individuals when new evidence arises in a case. Legislation should exist which would make it easier for practitioners to bring new information to the attention of the legal system and for the legal system to consider this new evidence. In the field of forensic pathology there can occasionally be a change in a case which could affect our interpretation and certification. The determination of manner of death may be based on the investigation and ancillary information gained by laboratory testing. The circumstances of a case are very important to our certification. If our knowledge of the circumstances change, such that the evidence no longer supports the manner of death as originally certified, a reconsideration of the manner may be required. Similarly, the practice of forensic pathology is based partly upon medical knowledge, which is constantly being reevaluated as medical science advances. New conditions may be discovered, or new clinical information may be disclosed at a later date which may influence the diagnosis, and thus the certification of cause or manner of death. It is important to accept that in light of new information reasonable people may appropriately change their mind and this process needs to be recognized by the legal system and courts to best serve the cause of justice.

Question 9. Should Congress require states to submit data on crime lab backlogs as a requisite for receiving Federal grant funding? If not, please explain why.

Answer. NAME supports requirements to address backlogs. Our current inspection and accreditation standards require that 90 percent of homicide cases are completed within 90 calendar days and 90 percent of all other cases be completed within 60 calendar days to be granted full NAME accreditation of an office or system. Our work to improve case turn-around-time would be aided by the establishment of similar standards for the toxicology labs which support our work. In many parts of the country families are unable to get autopsy reports death certificates in a timely manner due to months-years long delays in the receipt of toxicology testing.

Question 10. Does the Bureau of Justice Statistics (BJS) survey of public crime labs require states to assess their backlogs? If not, would this be an appropriate requirement?

Answer. This question is essentially directed at crime labs so NAME will not respond directly. The last BJS survey of medico-legal death investigation systems was conducted in 2002. A new and updated survey is long overdue and would be welcomed by the medico-legal death investigation community.

RESPONSE TO WRITTEN QUESTIONS SUBMITTED BY HON. JOHN D. ROCKEFELLER IV TO JILL SPRIGGS

Question 1. The National Academy of Sciences recommended that Congress create a new Federal agency to conduct rigorous, independent research and testing in the forensic sciences. If that isn't possible in the current budget climate, what other steps can Congress take to improve the science underpinning forensic techniques?

Answer. (A) Make funding specific toward a need and the application of the science—The National Academy of Forensic Sciences report demonstrated a need for and the development of a practical approach to research in regards to forensic science but first a specific roadmap or needs assessment must be created from the perspective of the end-user so as to ensure that funding can be directed to specific needs. Research would be most effective by enhancing ongoing efforts with established partners, such as colleges, universities, the national laboratory system, Scientific Working Groups, etc. and other Federal agencies. In the past, laboratories had the luxury of performing their own research, publishing the research and/or presenting the research. No longer do most crime labs have the option of performing research, since most are focused on rising backlogs in such disciplines as controlled substances, toxicology and latent prints. Who better to take the research created by universities and apply it to forensic disciplines than the scientists already working in the crime labs? Unfortunately, until backlogs are reduced, this will not happen.

(B) A Federal Repository is needed—Scientific Working Groups are an effective way of coordinating, managing and cataloging research efforts and a website should be created to perform as a repository of all research so that it is available for all to build on and utilize. This approach would help ensure research efforts are current and timely. We have already seen this call to action with Scientific Working Group for Firearms and Tool Marks (SWGGUN) and Scientific Working Group on Friction Ridge Analysis (SWGFAST). SWGFAST has always maintained that a significant body of constructive scientific research has already been conducted that addresses some of the concerns expressed in the National Academy of Sciences report.

(C) A review of existing research must be conducted—Since the release of the National Academy of Sciences report, additional research has been ongoing throughout the world which addresses the science of friction ridge identification. Some of that research has been published and/or reported on to the community, while some remains in progress. In November 2011, SWGFAST provided a 64 page response to a request from the Research, Development, Testing & Evaluation Inter-Agency Working Group of the National Science and Technology Council, Committee on Science, Subcommittee on Forensic Science asking for an annotated bibliography of the literature supporting the friction ridge sciences. This report available at *http://www.pdfdownload.org/pdf2html/pdf2html.php?url=http%3A%2F%2Fswgfast.org%2FResources%2F111117-ReplytoRDT%26E-FINAL.pdf&images=yes* was prepared on behalf of SWGFAST by a dedicated task force established at the University of Lausanne (Forensic Science Department of the Faculty of Law and Criminal Justice) under the direction of SWGFAST member Dr. Christophe Champod. Included within the report are publications covering the areas of: underlying fingerprint characteristics, minutiae sample sufficiency, fingerprint quality, fingerprint matching, type I and type II error, probability, analyst consideration, and end to end process reliability.

SWGGUN in their own regard compiled as part of the SWGGUN Admissibility Resource Kit (*www.swggun.org*) any research that has been performed to establish the validity of the forensic firearm and tool mark discipline. Numerous research projects have tested the fundamental propositions of the forensic firearm and tool mark discipline, resulting in the establishment and continued support of the AFTE Theory of Identification.

In response to questions posed by the Subcommittee on Forensic Science's Research, Development, Testing & Evaluation Interagency Working Group (RDT&E IWG), the SWGGUN compiled a list of annotated bibliographies of the foundational research performed in the forensic firearms and tool marks discipline. The list is 47 pages in length, and can be found on the SWGGUN website. *http://www.swggun.org/swg/index.php?option=com_content&view=article&id=51:swggun-responds-to-sofs-request&catid=13:other&Itemid=43*

The SWG groups could help facilitate the gathering, cataloging, storing, and disseminating existing research data, as well as research previously conducted and help in providing these materials to the community upon request and/or posting it on their specific website.

Question 2. In your testimony, you raised a concern that applying Federal Advisory Committee Act (FACA) regulations to the National Commission on Forensic Science will ensure that representatives from state and local forensic science organizations "do not have a voice in regards to any outcomes from the Commission." Given the Commission charter and the FACA provisions repeated below, can you further detail the reasoning behind this concern?

Answer. *Excerpt from the Charter of the DOJ National Commission on Forensic Justice*

> *12. Membership and Designation:* . . . The Commission members will be selected to achieve a balance of backgrounds, experiences, viewpoints, and expertise in scientific, legal, law enforcement, academic, and advocacy professions. Candidates for membership from non-federal entities will be solicited through the Federal Register and outreach to relevant professional societies.
>
> *Excerpt from the Federal Advisory Committee Act (5 U.S.C. App. 2.), as amended*
>
> *§ 10. Advisory committee procedures; meetings; notice, publication in Federal Register; regulations; minutes; certification; annual report; Federal officer or employee, attendance*
>
> (a)(1) Each advisory committee meeting shall be open to the public.
>
> (2) Except when the President determines otherwise for reasons of national security, timely notice of each such meeting shall be published in the Federal Register, and the Administrator shall prescribe regulations to provide for other types of public notice to insure that all interested persons are notified of such meeting prior thereto.
>
> (3) Interested persons shall be permitted to attend, appear before, or file statements with any advisory committee, subject to such reasonable rules or regulations as the Administrator may prescribe.

A few years ago, the National Science and Technology Council, Committee on Science conducted Interagency Working Groups (IWGs) via the Subcommittee on Forensic Science. The Subcommittee on Forensic Science was charged with the following tasks:

1. Develop a White Paper summarizing the Subcommittee on Forensic Science's recommendation to achieve the goals of the NRC report.
2. Create a prioritized national forensic science research agenda.

3. Draft a detailed strategy for developing and implementing common interoperability standards to facilitate the appropriate sharing of fingerprint data across technologies.

The IWGs were composed of federal, state and local forensic scientists, researchers and attorneys. At the end of 2012, the National Science and Technology Council was supposed to release a list of recommendations aimed at the forensic science community regarding five categories:

- Accreditation and Certification
- Education, Ethics and Terminology
- Standards, Practices and Protocols
- Outreach and Communications
- Research, Development, Testing and Evaluation

The forensic community has yet to see the release of these recommendations. Furthermore, the FACA provision was used as reasoning for the lack of communication throughout the forensic community in regards to the Interagency Working Groups (IWGs) and their development of these recommendations. Still to this day, the forensic community does not know the outcome of the information discussed or recommended as we near the completion of 2013.

Since the hearing, the forensic community has been assured by National Institute of Science and Technology (NIST) that state and local crime labs will have a voice in regards to the outcome of standards set by the Commission and FACA rules will reply. One distinction should be pointed out. While state and local crime laboratory directors on the Commission will have a voice, they will not be able to vote on any of the recommendations of the Commission. In addition, any standards handed down by the Commission will apply only to the Federal crime laboratories we have been told. State and local crime laboratories can adhere to these standards as they see fit. But one must remember, DNA CODIS and latent fingerprint databases are overseen by Federal agencies and because of this—a trickle-down effect of the standards voted on by the Commission must be adhered to by state and local crime laboratories in order to receive Federal grants and effectively participate in using these databases to solve crime in their geographical backyards.

Question 3. In raising concerns about new forensic science standards, your testimony seemed to express support for the ongoing Scientific Working Group (SWG) standard development process. However, as I mentioned during the hearing, Judge Harry Edwards, who co-chaired the panel responsible for the Strengthening Forensic Sciences report, has criticized the SWGs for being of questionable value in that they meet irregularly, lack membership standards, and generate vague, unenforceable guidelines without measuring progress against them. How would your organization respond to these criticisms? What elements of the SWGs is your organization most supportive of?

Answer. On February 15, 2013 an announcement was made by the Department of Justice (DOJ) and National Institute of Standards and Technology (NIST) establishing a National Commission on Forensic Science that will consist of a thirty member "commission" as well as discipline specific "guidance groups". The guidance groups will develop and propose discipline specific recommendations, and the Commission will consider whether to endorse and recommend those guidelines and if they are to be implemented for use.

The precursor groups to these "guidance groups" are twenty-one existing Scientific Working Groups (SWGs). SWGs (originally "TWGs") have been representing the rich and diverse array of the forensic sciences since TWGDAM (now SWGDAM) was formed in 1988. Since that time, the number of SWGS has grown in order to remain current with emerging disciplines and the constant evolution of forensic science. These SWGs have worked to standardize and advance the practices of their disciplines for more than twenty years; producing concrete results through the publication of hundreds of documents that provide clear recommendations and guidance in forensic science. The success of the SWGS' work is evident by citations in countless judicial proceedings. The SWGs are recognized by their international counterparts as leaders in the global forensic community as well as leaders in research and development.

The criticisms of Judge Harry Edwards, who co-chaired the panel responsible for the *Strengthening Forensic Sciences* report, reflect information that was not complete and needs further discussion. The lack of information stems from the fact that the NAS Committee did not engage with ALL of the SWGs. Had they done so, they would have learned that the criticisms reflected in the report, while potentially valid for some SWGs, are not valid for the majority.

Irregular meetings: It is a valid criticism that many SWGs meet irregularly. But SWGs that have had consistent funding do meet regularly and produce more standards and guideline documents than those who do not. It is clear that constant and consistent funding for each SWG is critical for their success. With the onset of sequestration, most SWGs have been adversely affected, having meetings reduced or cancelled. An oversight organization which operates all of the SWGs, and provides sufficient funding to support regular meetings by all SWGs, would adequately address this criticism.

Membership standards: Well-run SWGs have clear bylaws which delineate such areas as membership requirements. The majority of the SWGs do have clearly delineated bylaws and membership standards. The creation of an oversight organization which operates all of the SWGs and could ensure that membership guidelines are established for all SWGs, would adequately address this criticism. Note, however, that the membership standards which may be appropriate for one SWG may not be so for all; therefore flexibility in developing these standards must exist to address the needs of each SWG.

Unenforceable guidelines—The SWGs as currently formed exist within the forensic community and are well known by their practitioners. There is no regulatory force that is associated with them (including their creation). They were created by members of the forensic community to address recognized needs within their disciplines for best practices and guidelines. The SWGs have never been "granted" any authority to create or enforce these guidelines or standards by any official regulatory body. The guidelines produced are distributed to members of their respective forensic community to solicit feedback to make sure the guidelines are useful by all and appropriate for the discipline. It is the members of the forensic community that have supported and endorsed these guidelines.

SWG documents have been cited in court proceedings and many SWGs keep track of how often their documents have been cited in court proceedings. The courts have been responsible in many cases of "enforcing" the standards by recognizing the validity of individual SWG documents when accepting testimony. In addition, some SWGs have gone through the process of having their documents published under standards organizations such as ASTM. In the event that an oversight organization is created which operates all of the SWGs, and this organization be given some authority over implementation of those standards, then this criticism would also be addressed.

The SWGs have long provided the necessary scientific guidance needed by the forensic community. If the needs of the SWG groups are met with consistent funding and administrative support, we are convinced that the concerns of the NAS report will be addressed. With the advent of a single funding and organizational body, all twenty-one current Scientific Working Groups—representing the breadth of forensic science—will be able to come together under one organization to continue their work advancing the forensic sciences. By uniting, there is clearly an opportunity for the SWGs to become even more successful and to continue to provide their community the necessary guidance for years to come.

○

www.ingramcontent.com/pod-product-compliance
Lightning Source LLC
Chambersburg PA
CBHW081218170526
45165CB00009B/2864